MOZART AND GREAT MUSIC

A Lifetime of Learning, Book 4

Mark Andre Alexander

Make clear distinctions,
and examine all things well.
*The Golden Verses of
Pythagoras*

THE SCHOOL OF
PYTHAGORAS™

Auburn, CA

Published by Mark Andre Alexander
P.O. Box 5286, Auburn, CA 95604-5286

First Edition, Version 2_2

Library of Congress Cataloging-in-Publication Data

Alexander, Mark Andre, 1956-
Mozart and great music: a lifetime of learning, book 4 / by Mark Andre Alexander

p. cm. — (A Lifetime of Learning Series: Book 4)
ISBN 978-1-937597-24-5

An Amazon.Com Kindle eBook

Cover design by Melinda De Ross: www.coveredbymelinda.com

Photos and illustrations are created by the author, in the public domain, or licensed from ThinkStock.com˝, Photos.com˝, PhotoDisc˙, and Nova Development Corporation.

Formatted for iPad and other tablets. (Amazon links may not work on Apple products. Go to MarkAndreAlexander.Com to access a free 36-day course on Creating Your Life.)

Thanks to Bree, Scott, Kas, Keith, and Christina. Also, thanks to Frank Weeden for fine copyediting and BubbleCow.Com for great book editing, both services at a reasonable price.

Subscribe to the "Creating Your Life" channel on YouTube. Check out One-Click-To-Mozart page at:
MarkAndreAlexander.com/one-click-to-mozart

Also by Mark Andre Alexander

Creating Your Life (A Lifetime of Learning, Book 1)
Money and Wealth (A Lifetime of Learning, Book 2)
Sex and Romance (A Lifetime of Learning, Book 3)

Handbook for Advanced Souls: Eternal Reminders for the Present Moment

Public domain works edited by Mark Andre Alexander

Hamlet and the Scottish Succession by Lilian Winstanley
Shakespeare's Law and Latin by Sir George Greenwood, M.P.
The George Greenwood Collection

For Bree and HK,
and those who Quest

CONTENTS

About This Series

How many times have we said it to ourselves?

If I only knew then what I knew now?

This series of little books, titled *A Lifetime of Learning*, gives my personal, and admittedly idiosyncratic, discoveries over the years. I wish I had these gems in my teens. Discoveries, I now find, most adults still seem to have missed.

Of course, I may not have acted on that knowledge, but still it would have been nice to know. In many cases, knowing then what I know now would have saved me time, money, and heartache, would have enriched me, and would have given me greater personal freedom.

As a child and youngster, I had five years of training in classical piano. One of my first experiences playing piano was Mozart. But not until I was a college-aged adult did I begin to fully appreciate Mozart.

All I knew for sure is that, during those few years of training in classical piano, I loved playing Mozart.

Each chapter has an associated Chapter Playlist on YouTube. This allows you to access all the videos for that chapter in one place.

The publishing imprint I have chosen for this series, The School of Pythagoras, points to the quest for the fundamental nature of Truth.

This series is dedicated to those of you on that quest.

Introduction

"The meaning of music lies not in the fact
that it is too vague for words,
but that it is too precise for words."
Felix Mendelssohn

Playlist 0: MarkAndreAlexander.com/One-Click-to-Mozart/
(6 videos, 43 min)

If you learn one thing only from this little book, then let it be
this:

You can directly experience
heavenly states of consciousness
listening to Mozart.

Contrary to popular belief, truly Great Art (such as that
created by a Shakespeare, a Mozart, a Michelangelo, a Sesshu, an
al-Mutanabbi) is more objectively great than most people realize,
not just a matter of subjective opinion.

True, some people have preferences that may exclude Great Art. They may even have profound, sublime experiences with the works of artists that appear simplistic and trite to others.

Some insist that Pachelbel's *Canon in D*, a favorite at weddings, is heavenly:

Video 1: Pachelbel: *Canon in D*

Pachelbel's Canon *can* be moving and beautiful.

But it is not objectively Great Art. Not in a world that includes Mozart. Is this merely my subjective view? We will see in Chapter 1. But first, one question must be answered:

What makes Great Art great? The answer, paradoxically, points to how Great Art induces in someone rare and powerful *subjective* experiences.

Great Art transports one into realms that makes one wonder, "How is it possible that a mere human being created that?"

Great Art can imbue a spiritual revelation each time one experiences it.

Great Art carves out states of consciousness that transcend the human.

Great Art embodies an eternal mystery.

Great Art catalyzes, transforms, and transfigures.

And more often than not, Great Art requires you to meet its demands before it unlocks its transfiguring mystery.

People who have never tried to meet the demands of Great Art (through education or training), or who have tried but stopped before the door opened, may call all art a matter of opinion. They may believe it all to be mere preference, without one preference being greater than any other.

Not true.

Pachelbel's *Canon in D* may provide extraordinary pleasure for some, but it cannot possibly be defined as Great Art. The same can be said for most popular music today.

> *These works do not transport one into realms*
> *that makes one wonder, "How is it possible*
> *that a mere human being created that?"*

Don't get me wrong. I spend more time listening to popular music than music that is Great Art. I love jazz, pop, ambient, rock, metal, alternative, and many genres beyond and in between.

I love The Beatles, John Coltrane, The Cars, Evanescence, Brian Eno, Ella Fitzgerald, Enya, Led Zeppelin, U2, Al Di Meola, Fever Ray, Robbie Williams, Devin Townsend, Steve Morse, Yes, Cirque du Soleil, Jon Mark, Peter Murphy, Rodney Jones, Larry Siegel, Dean Martin, Todd Rundgren, Adele, Blue Oyster Cult, Keith Jarrett, and many more artists.

But rarely do their creations rise to Great Art. (Occasionally, in my view, some jazz greats achieve it, like John Coltrane, Charlie Bird, and Dizzy Gillespie.)

Examples of Great Art include the likes of the already famous *Eine kleine Nachtmusik* (A Little Night Music), 1ˢᵗ

Movement *allegro*. (The "K" stands for the Köchel number, created by Ludwig Ritter von Köchel, who catalogued the works.)

> **Video 2: K. 525: *Serenade No. 13 in G, "Eine kleine nachtmusik"* (I. Allegro, with score)**

Or the achingly beautiful 2nd movement of Mozart's *Piano Concerto No. 21*. This video with an animated graph helps you "visually hear" the individual instruments.

> **Video 3: K. 467: *Piano Concerto No. 21 in C* (II. Andante)**

Or the groundbreaking *Symphony No. 40 in G minor*. (The term "G minor" refers to the musical key in which the symphony is composed.)

> **Video 4: K. 550: *Symphony No. 40 in G minor* (I. Molto Allegro)**

These pieces of music have been played so much that, as beautiful and profound as they are, they have almost become cliché. So we will focus on other music, less popularized, to achieve some freshness in recognizing Mozart's heavenly beauty.

Among the many composers who consistently create Great Art, Mozart stands alone. The unique Danish comedian, conductor and pianist Victor Borge, sums it up best:

> *"I always thought that if you went to heaven,*
> *you would meet all the great people;*
> *anybody who came up there*
> *would all gather in huge rooms.*
> *But Mozart has a room all by himself."*

The great conductor and pianist Daniel Barenboim gives us in these two short videos a description of how to begin telling the difference.

Video 5: "How to Listen to Music" by Daniel Barenboim

Video 6: Barenboim Talks about Music

How This Little Book Can Help

The aim of this book is simple—to give you a direct personal experience with a heavenly state of consciousness while listening to Mozart's music.

Or if you already have access to Mozart's heavenly mansion, to provide you a glimpse into more rooms within that mansion, with greater appreciation.

Fortunately, YouTube provides all the musical examples we need to unlock the doors to the mansion. Throughout this book, I will link to YouTube videos that offer inspired performances. And inspired performances make a difference.

Mark Twain once said:

> *"The difference between the right word*
> *and the almost right word*
> *is the difference between the lightning*
> *and the lightning bug.*

And so it is with great music:

> *The difference between the right performance*
> *and the almost right performance*

is the difference between heaven
and a dictionary definition of heaven.

Also, at the beginning of each chapter I provide a link to the
YouTube playlist that includes all the pieces of music mentioned in
that chapter in order. (Note: If a video becomes unavailable, an
alternative can usually be found by searching YouTube using the
Köchel number.)

Links to the playlists, and much more, are also available at:

MarkAndreAlexander.com/One-Click-to-Mozart/

Listening to inspired performances is crucial.

Not all recordings are inspired.
Not all do Mozart justice.

But lucky for us, intrepid lovers of Mozart have made
available many of the performances I had hoped to find.

But be aware of the limitations.

Mozart's music, like all great music,
is best experienced by an inspired live performance
in a great concert hall or chamber venue.

Next best, on a great sound system in stereo. Or on
headphones.

Therefore, YouTube can only offer a small experience of that
heaven. Be prepared to track down and purchase inspired
recordings, recommended by me or by some of the guides listed
in "Recommended Readings and Recordings" near the end of the
book.

Here's a glimpse into what follows:

Chapter 1: Why Is Mozart Great? surveys what people from several professions think of Mozart, indicating a broad appeal.

Chapter 2: Hearing Mozart, Part 1: Serenade No. 10 for Winds, "Gran Partita" focuses on one piece of chamber music to illustrate how Mozart provides a harmonic approach to music rather than a purely melodic one.

Chapter 3: Mozart—The Child, the Myth, the Man details his childhood accomplishments while also subverting the man-child myth.

Chapter 4: Hearing Mozart, Part 2: The Magic Flute, Overture extends the idea of listening to Mozart differently in a harmonic, multi-level way, even when he is composing something especially melodic.

Chapter 5: Mozart's Piano Concertos covers some of Mozart's greatest contributions to music, pitting a solo pianist against an orchestra, foreshadowing a composer like Beethoven who extends the distinction even further.

Chapter 6: Hearing Mozart, Part 3: Sinfonia Concertante in E-flat introduces the idea of musical rhetoric, and classical music as oration and conversation.

Chapter 7: Mozart's Chamber Music: "A Blessing of Inconceivable Richness" strives to illuminate Mozart's incredible range of music for small ensembles: sonatas for two players, trios, quartets, and quintets.

Chapter 8: Hearing Mozart, Part 4: Singular, Idiosyncratic, and Special-Occasion Gems surveys a range of unusual compositions that illustrate Mozart's wide range of musical interests.

Chapter 9: Mozart's Symphonies surveys symphonies, with greatest emphasis on his final one, the "Jupiter."

Chapter 10: Hearing Mozart, Part 5: Symphony No. 40 in G minor dives deep into a symphony regarded as Mozart's finest.

Chapter 11: Mozart and Opera: Le nozze di Figaro (The Marriage of Figaro) touches on his seven great operas, with the great *The Marriage of Figaro* as the main attraction, thought by many to be one of the finest comic operas of all time.

Chapter 12: Mozart's Heavenly Mansion provides a special listening session of heavenly musical architecture.

Next you will find "The *Mozart and Great Music* Checklist" and "Recommended Readings and Recordings." There is also an appendix that a list of Mozart's four-star compositions.

Several chapters include an "Extended Discussion" section for readers interested in going more deeply into a particular piece of music or some other musical fundamentals.

The recommendations in this book, faithfully applied, *do* deliver. They will help you experience Mozart's heavenly music in ways that may transfigure and transform you.

So let's begin this marvelous musical adventure.

Chapter 1

Why Is Mozart Great?

*"Neither a lofty degree of intelligence nor imagination
nor both together go to the making of genius.
Love, love, love, that is the soul of genius."*
Mozart

Playlist 1: MarkAndreAlexander.com/One-Click-to-Mozart/
(3 videos, 17 min)

*"In art there is Leonardo da Vinci, in literature there is
Shakespeare, in music there is Mozart."* **Itzhak Perlman**

Why is Mozart great?

Louis Armstrong was once asked, "What is jazz?"

He answered, "Man, if you have to ask what it is, you'll never know." Perhaps he would have said something similar about Mozart. But I think we can attempt a partial answer.

Violinist Itzhak Perlman puts Mozart in the company of Shakespeare and Leonardo da Vinci. And with good reason. Let's look at Shakespeare and da Vinci.

Shakespeare seems to have surveyed the entire human experience, emotional and intellectual, in his drama and poetry. Later writers see Shakespeare as the banquet of writing in the English language, and they are left taking mere crumbs from his table. In other words, Shakespeare makes later writers feel like there is little left to write about.

One academic, Harold Bloom in his book *Shakespeare: The Invention of the Human*, goes so far as to claim that, in Western culture, Shakespeare has created humans as we know them today.

Da Vinci is the polymath who makes other polymaths appear normal. He transcends as a painter, sculptor, architect, writer, mathematician, engineer, inventor, anatomist, geologist, cartographer, and botanist. He climbed several artistic peaks.

Mozart climbed a musical peak during the Classical era (1730-1820). Unlike many artists today, he was not much interested in charting out his own territory. Like Shakespeare before him, he took what already existed and refined it into greatness. And those who follow feel like there is little left for them.

That's why beginning in the Romantic era (1780-1910) we begin seeing composers shift into approaching art as self-expression, trying to chart out new territory that has not been conquered.

The end-result in the twentieth century includes works like John Cage's classical work *4:33* in which four members of a quartet come on stage and sit, playing nothing, for four minutes and thirty-three seconds. Or extremely dissonant atonal music that requires educated listeners for full appreciation.

> *All three—Mozart, Shakespeare, and Da Vinci—*
> *are singular in their respective arts.*
> *To others they appear more than human.*

As American biographer Robert Gutman says of Mozart,

> *"Like all geniuses of his rank,*
> *he stands as a law to himself:*
> *incommensurable, incalculable, sublime."*

But Why Mozart?

Some may wonder why I've chosen Mozart rather than Bach, Haydn, or Beethoven.

First some background and dates.

There were four great musical periods in Western classical music before modern and contemporary music. I've included a few of the great composers of each period:

1. Baroque era, 1600-1760
Claudio Monteverdi (1567-1643)
Antonio Vivaldi (1678-1741)
George Frederic Handel (1685-1759)
Johann Sebastian Bach (1685-1750)

2. Classical era, 1730-1820
Joseph Haydn (1732-1809)
Wolfgang Amadeus Mozart (1756-1791)
Ludwig van Beethoven (1770-1827)
Franz Schubert (1797-1828)

3. Romantic era, 1780-1910
Hector Berlioz (1803-1869)
Felix Mendelssohn (1809-1847)
Frederic Chopin (1810-1849)
Franz Liszt (1811-1886)
Richard Wagner (1813-1883)
Giuseppe Verdi (1813-1901)
Johannes Brahms (1833-1897)
Pyotr Ilyich Tchaikovsky (1840-1893)

4. Impressionist era, 1875-1925
Claude Debussy (1862-1918)
Maurice Ravel (1875-1937)
Frederick Delius (1862-1934)
Ottorino Respighi (1879-1936)

Among all of these great composers who composed Great Art, Mozart stands unique.

How?

Perhaps the only way to get at the answer in words is to see how various musicians, composers, conductors, biographers, and philosophers have attempted to explain Mozart. No other composer generates the kinds of responses that Mozart did.

Two words keep coming up when people speak of Mozart. The first word is some form of the word *perfect*.

> *"There is nothing **perfect** in this world except Mozart's music."*
> Thomas Love Peacock, English novelist and poet

> *"Mozart tapped the source from which all music flows, expressing himself with a spontaneity and refinement and breathtaking rightness. What we expect to find in Mozart is **perfection** in whatever medium he chose to work."*
> Aaron Copland, American composer and conductor

"*Mozart's music is on the one hand so accessible,
so beautiful and so apparently simple that it can be grasped. But at
the same time and enjoyed on its first hearing, it is so deep, so
profound, so* **perfect** *that one can spend a lifetime in it
and continue to be fascinated with it,
even if it's the hundredth time you've performed it.*"
James Conlon, American conductor

"*He is up to the present the most* **perfect** *manifestation
of musical talent... His sense of form is almost superhuman.
Like a masterpiece of sculpture or art, his art,
viewed from any side, is a* **perfect** *picture.*"
Ferruccio Busoni, Italian composer

"*When it comes to Mozart, you're speaking of the most
extraordinary* **perfection** *that exists. There isn't anything that is
more* **perfect** *in music. And then on top of it the music is so
complete; there is never a piece of music by Mozart,
it doesn't make any difference if he is 4, 5, 6, or 26,
it's* **perfect**, *totally* **perfect**.*"
Pinchas Zukerman, Israeli violinist and conductor

"*It is hard to think of another composer
who so* **perfectly** *marries form and passion.*"
Leonard Bernstein, American composer and conductor

"*As an artist, as a musician, Mozart was not a man of this world.
To a certain part of the 19th century his work seemed
to possess so pure, so formally rounded, so 'godlike' a* **perfection**
*that Richard Wagner, the most violent spokesman of the Romantic
Period, could call him 'music's genius of light and love.'*"
Alfred Einstein, German-American biographer

The second word that keeps coming up when people speak
of Mozart is some form of the word *beauty*. Not just that the
music he writes is beautiful, but also that the music itself
somehow embodies the ideal of beauty, the thing itself.

*"Mozart's music is so **beautiful** as to entice angels down to earth."*
Franz Alexander von Kleist, German poet

*"Mozart is the greatest composer of all. Beethoven created his music, but the music of Mozart is of such purity and **beauty** that one feels he merely found it—that it has always existed as part of the inner **beauty** of the universe waiting to be revealed."*
Albert Einstein, German-born physicist and violinist

*"Mozart does not give the listener time to catch his breath, for no sooner is one inclined to reflect upon a **beautiful** inspiration then another appears, even more splendid, which drives away the first, and this continues on and on, so that in the end one is unable to retain any of these **beauties** in the memory."*
Karl Ditters von Dittersdorf, Austrian composer and violinist

*"He is the most generous composer who ever lived. He showered upon us melody after melody, character upon character, **beauty**, upon **beauty**."*
Robert Harris, English music critic

*"What was evident was that Mozart was simply transcribing music completely finished in his head. And finished as most music is never finished. Displace one note and there would be diminishment. Displace one phrase and structure would fall. I was staring through the cage of those meticulous ink strokes at Absolute **Beauty**."*
Peter Shaffer, English playwright (*Amadeus*)

*"In Mozart's music, all intensity are crystallized in the clearest, the most **beautifully** balanced and proportioned, and altogether flawless musical forms. For one moment in the history of music all opposites were reconciled; all tensions resolved; that luminous moment was Mozart."*
Phil Goulding, American classical music journalist

*"Mozart's mature instrumental music represents
our civilization's sign for the **beautiful**. We cannot think of him
without thinking of **beauty**; we cannot refer to **beauty** without
recalling his music. I believe this is so, not necessarily because his
works are more **beautiful** than those of other composers, though
this may well be true, but because he created—or, at least, brought
into the forefront of aesthetic consciousness—a special kind of
beauty, one that thenceforth came to exemplify the idea of
superlative **beauty** itself."*
Maynard Solomon, American musicologist and biographer

*"If we cannot write with the **beauty** of Mozart,
let us at least try to write with his purity."*
Johannes Brahms, German composer

But there's more...

When speaking of Mozart, more than any other composer,
people are likely to invoke heaven, the divine, God, miracles, or
some other reference to, or experience of, the ultimate.

*"Mozart has reached the boundary gate of music
and leaped over it, leaving behind the old masters
and moderns, and posterity itself."*
Alexander Hyatt King, English Mozart scholar

*"The Mozartian legacy, in brief, is as good
an excuse for mankind's existence as
we shall ever encounter and is perhaps, after all,
a still small hope for our ultimate survival."*
H. C. Robbins Landon, American musicologist

*"Mozart's music is the mysterious language
of a distant spiritual kingdom,
whose marvelous accents echo in our inner being
and arouse a higher, intensive life."*
E.T.A. Hoffmann, German author, composer, music critic

"The most tremendous genius raised Mozart above all masters,
in all centuries and in all arts."
Richard Wagner, German composer

"Mozart is an utterly unique phenomenon,
indisputably and forever on the
credit side of life's ledger, so sovereign
and omnipresent that he reconciles
us somewhat to the debit side.
Indeed, Mozart seems to be reconciliation
itself, a kind of redeeming miracle."
Wolfgang Hildesheimer, German biographer

"Mozart resolved his emotions on a level
that transformed them into moods
uncontaminated by mortal anguish,
enabling him to express the angelic anguish
that is so peculiarly his own."
Yehudi Menuhin, American-born violinist and conductor

"In Bach, Beethoven and Wagner
we admire principally the depth
and energy of the human mind;
in Mozart, the divine instinct."
Edvard Grieg, Norwegian composer

"Mozart exists, and will exist, eternally;
divine Mozart—less a name, more a soul
descending to us from the heavens."
Charles Gounod, French composer

"Mozart's joy is made of serenity,
and a phrase of his music is like a
calm thought; his simplicity is merely purity.
It is a crystalline thing in which
all the emotions play a role, but as if
already celestially transposed."
André Gide, Nobel Prize-winning French author

"Mozart makes you believe in God because it cannot be by chance that such a phenomenon arrives into this world and leaves such an unbounded number of unparalleled masterpieces."
Georg Solti, Hungarian conductor

"It is thanks to Mozart that I have devoted my life to music... Mozart is the highest, the culminating point that beauty has attained in the sphere of music. Mozart is the musical Christ."
Piotr Tchaikovsky Russian composer

"This is the music that they are going to play for me when I enter heaven, or wherever Mozart may be."
Marcel Maurice,
French clarinetist on Mozart's *Quintet for Clarinet in A*

"The angels, left to themselves, play Mozart, and the dear Lord likes especially to listen to them then."
Karl Barth, Swiss philosopher

"Others may reach heaven with their works. But Mozart, he comes from there."
Joseph Krips, Austrian conductor and violinist

"Once, when filling out an application for a summer job, on that line next to 'other' under the heading of Religion, I wrote Mozart. The personnel officer was not amused, but then, I hadn't intended it as a joke. For there was a time when I was convinced that Mozart was at least as divinely inspired as Moses, Christ, the Buddha, Lao-tzu, or Mohammed, and I suppose I still am. For in no other works of the human imagination can the divine spirit be heard more distinctly than in the miraculous music this often vulgar, unpleasant, and difficult man produced during his pathetically brief thirty-five years. Were this book to do him justice, the section devoted to Mozart's music would take up more than half the total pages."
Jim Svejda, American music critic, in the
3rd edition of *The Record Shelf Guide to the Classical Repertoire*

Are these writers over the top in their praise? Perhaps.

But there is something about Mozart's music, given enough time and exposure, that elicits such intense reactions.

In the movie *The Shawshank Redemption*, there is a scene where an innocent man convicted of his wife's murder goes into the warden's office and locks everyone out.

Why?

To play a Mozart *duettino* (a song with two singers) for himself, and eventually, to play it for the entire prison population. Watch what happens:

> **Video 1: "Duettino - Sull'aria" from *Le nozze di Figaro* (The Marriage of Figaro), from *The Shawshank Redemption***

Mozart, when conveyed through inspired performances, is capable of a kind of transport, a sublime movement, into a heavenly experience that transcends physical, emotional, and mental limitations.

Where others are loved for the mental and emotional craft of their music, with occasional passages and moments that arrive in heaven, Mozart appears to naturally dwell there.

Here's one of the best examples of how a great composer takes listeners on a journey into a heavenly world of emotional and noble passions. In Beethoven's *Symphony No. 5 in C minor*, the transition at the end of the 3rd movement into the 4th movement marks one of the finest transitions ever composed into one of the most heavenly final movements ever.

> **Video 2: Beethoven: *Symphony No. 5 in D minor*, 4th Movement *Allegro***

Mozart does not take one on a journey to heaven as much as he is already resident there at the start, unlike so many of his fellow musical composers.

And thus Mozart is unique among musical artists. He is the Shakespeare, the Michelangelo, the Da Vinci of music.

Perhaps there is no way to explain Mozart. Perhaps all we can do is accept the inevitable, as expressed by one Japanese classical pianist and conductor:

"Mozart is inexplicable."
Mitsuko Uchida

But we are going to give it a try.

One thing to keep in mind is that musicians and conductors can look at a musical score and *hear the music* as they read the notes. Just as you can read a novel and *hear* people talk or see what they are doing.

Musical notation is a real language
with as much variety and communication
as the words, sentences, and
subtle meanings written on this page.

Let's watch Salieri's reaction to Mozart's manuscripts in the movie *Amadeus* as he *reads* the scores and *hears* the music:

Video 3: Salieri's reaction to Mozart's manuscripts, from *Amadeus*

What is Salieri hearing? What moves him so profoundly? He knows that what he is hearing is the Divine Voice, and sadly, that he will never get as close to it.

In the next chapter, we focus on one musical example, going more deeply into key aspects of one work. In this way, you will begin to hear things you have not heard before, and you will capture a better picture of what a composer is capable of doing with such an abstract thing as music.

The chapters on *Hearing Mozart* may be more challenging for some readers. But your efforts will be rewarded. With a little bit of close listening, we can begin training your ear to hear in new ways.

Chapter 2

Hearing Mozart, Part 1: *Serenade No. 10 in B-flat for Winds, "Gran Partita"*

"On the page it looked nothing. The beginning simple, almost comic. Just a pulse—bassoons and basset horns—like a rusty squeezebox. Then suddenly—high above it—an oboe, a single note, hanging there unwavering, till a clarinet took over and sweetened it into a phrase of such delight! This was no composition by a performing monkey! This was a music I'd never heard. Filled with such longing, such unfulfillable longing, it had me trembling. It seemed to me that I was hearing the very voice of God." Salieri in the film *Amadeus*, on the 3rd movement of Mozart's *Serenade No. 10 in B-flat for Winds*

Playlist 2: MarkAndreAlexander.com/One-Click-to-Mozart/ (4 videos, 1 hr 13 min)

If we cannot explain Mozart, at least we can listen to him and grasp what is inexplicable by directly experiencing his music.

Take a few minutes and listen to the music Salieri describes in the opening quote. The musical score below shows the first 38 seconds of music:

Video 1: K. 361: *Serenade No. 10 in B-flat for Winds* **(Gran Partita, III. Adagio)**

For the first 24 seconds (24s) Mozart sets the stage with a kind of rhythmic heartbeat. Listen again to those 24s.

You can hear the systolic (contracting) and diastolic (expanding) actions of a heart pumping in, out, and then resting. Mozart uses several kinds of basset horns for this effect, but also a second oboe and a second clarinet.

At 24s the oboe comes in—a high, pure, and gentle melody.

Then at 36s, the clarinet takes over the melody, and fits it in with the heartbeat.

Listen again to the first 60s of the music.

One of Mozart's great strengths is his ability to create music that displays like a multi-faceted jewel.

Mozart's music is reflective,
showing brilliant musical mirrors of light,
with different facets.

Let's focus on one simple example of this mirroring effect.

Start at 60s (01:00).

At 01:07 the clarinet plays a rise and fall in the melody.

Then at 01:11, before the previous melody concludes, Mozart plays the same melody with a basset horn (an instrument like a clarinet but with a deeper sound).

Then at 01:15 for the third time Mozart's plays the melody, but with the higher oboe. And he adds a new facet by running the melody through more notes.

This simple yet masterful play of melody, overlapping across instruments, is one key to Mozart's brilliance and beauty.

Mozart plays with melodies
the way children play with bubbles.

While Mozart's *Serenade No. 13 in G, "Eine kleine Nachtmusik"* is an example of Mozart's supreme talent with melodic music, this movement in Mozart's *Serenade No. 10 in B-flat for Winds* is an example of Mozart's supreme talent with *harmonic* music that plays off the melodies with multiple layers and development.

If you listen to the entire movement with this idea in mind, you will begin to hear how Mozart continually plays with different instruments reflecting the music. It's more than just melody. It's the interplay among the instruments and musical lines, what is implied between them.

In fact, at the end of the piece, you probably could not remember enough of the melody to hum it all the way through. (Unlike the 1st movement of *Eine Kleine Nachtmusik.*)

And as you get to know the music more deeply from multiple hearings, the full jewel emerges.

The more you know by heart a piece by Mozart,
the more you enter a timeless realm where
the full jewel-like music emerges and pierces your heart.

Let me explain what I mean...

Think of one of your favorite songs, one that you know every lyric and every moment of its music. Remember the first time you heard it?

Perhaps you did not fully like it. But with repeated hearings, it grew inside you.

Now you can practically play the entire song in your head. And when you can do this, something else happens when you hear the song.

The song plays out of time.

What I mean is, at each moment while listening, you know everything that has come before and everything that is coming next in the song.

You can know, while listening to an early lyric in the song, that later the same lyric comes back with a slight difference. And you feel that, while listening to the early lyric.

When you listen to the same song over and over again, you begin hearing all of its levels at one time.

If it's a rock song, you can listen through the song focused on the lyrics and the singer. The next time, you can switch focus and follow the guitars. Then the next time you can switch focus onto the bass or the drums.

You are able to separate the elements that come together to make a song and appreciate the brilliance of each.

You begin to *know* the song so well that you can shift your attention *while listening,* moving from vocals to instruments and back, reflecting on the lyrical and musical meanings.

> *And each time you listen to it,*
> *you gain new musical experiences.*

In the beginning, you have a linear *melodic* experience with the song.

Later, you start to have a nonlinear, wholistic *harmonic* experience with the song.

At every given moment of the song, the reflection of the *entire* song is in your heart and mind.

You know the song so deeply, that you know it as a *whole.*

Mozart composed in total. He composed as if he were hearing the entire thing, all at once, from beginning to end.

He composed music as a *whole*.

> *Somehow when Mozart composed,*
> *he heard the music outside of time and space,*
> *the first time.*

Let's close with Salieri's actual description of the opening of this heavenly piece of music in the film *Amadeus*:

Video 2: Salieri's reaction to Mozart's *Serenade for Winds in B-flat major, Gran Partita, 3rd movement, Adagio, from *Amadeus

The film *Amadeus* itself portrays Mozart as a kind of man-child, a spoiled boy who did not have an adult's sense of the world. The film is not a true reflection of Mozart.

However, the movie still works because it helps the audience experience the true transport of Mozart's music.

The *whole* music.

The Mozart Effect and Healing

In 1997 Don Campbell published *The Mozart Effect*. When people hear this, they think Campbell claimed that children raised listening to Mozart help children become smarter. Campbell's actual suggestions, based on anecdotal evidence, are more specific: that music of the Viennese Classical period can connect with those who are mentally isolated from people, such as those with autism, and can help infants react and think better.

He also claimed that the music of Mozart in particular contributes to improved working of the higher brain functions, especially logical and mathematical concepts.

Although Campbell's work is not science, interesting anecdotal evidence does point to Mozart's music contributing to increased mental health.

Pioneering French listening researcher Alfred Tomatis, author of *The Conscious Ear*, studied how erroneous hearing could be the root cause of a variety of ailments. He believed that speech problems are often related to personal family problems and oral communication issues that can arise. One of his most famous patients was the French actor Gerard Depardieu.

> In the mid-1960s, Depardieu was a tongue-tied young man still struggling to become an actor. He came from a dysfunctional family with several personal tragedies, and experienced educational failures. He wanted to be an actor but stammered when trying to express himself.
>
> He came to the Tomatis Center and Dr. Tomatis determined that Depardieu's voice and memory problems resulted from deep emotional problems.
>
> Depardieu asked what could be done to help him, and the doctor's reply amazed him: "For the next several weeks, I want you to come here every day for two hours and listen to Mozart."
>
> Depardieu started the next day listening to Mozart on headphones. After only a few sessions, his appetite improved, he slept better, and he

experienced more energy.

Soon he began speaking more clearly. Months later, he returned to acting school demonstrating a new confidence, grace, and bearing. He is now highly regarded as one of the great actors of his generation.

"Before Tomatis," Depardieu said, "I could not complete any of my sentences. He helped give continuity to my thoughts, and he gave me the power to synthesize and understand what I was thinking."

Extended Discussion

If you get the recording of the *Serenade No. 10 in B-flat for Winds* by Neville Marriner (the version used in *Amadeus*), listen to it in stereo or on headphones with your eyes closed.

> *Mozart composes spatially.*
> *His music is architecture.*

Listen to the arc of instruments, how the melody moves across instruments in space, mainly in the oboe, clarinet, and basset horn, but also reflected in the other instruments. Harmonically, Mozart hears music both in time and space, not only horizontally with how the performers are arranged, but also vertically in how the music lays out on the score.

> *You don't have to read music*
> *to spot the patterns of notes on a score.*

Rarely is there a piece of music that relies almost solely on so many horns and reed instruments. The entire Serenade in seven movements ranks as one of Mozart's best works and worthy of your time.

Here's a recording with Charles Mackerras conducting.

Video 3: K. 361: *Serenade No. 10 in B-flat for Winds* (Gran Partita, complete)

Here are the seven movements and their start times so you can skip to any of them for a listen.

00:00 - Largo. Allegro molto
09:14 - Menuetto - Trio I - Trio II
19:31 - Adagio
25:02 - Menuetto. Allegretto - Trio I - Trio II
30:24 - Romanze. Adagio - Allegretto - Adagio
37:45 - Thema mit Variationen
47:18 - Rondo. Allegro molto

The 5th and 6th movements are especially notable for their heavenly qualities. With the 6th movement, notice how the opening variations convey a cheerful and carefree air. Later the variations begin to soften, deepen, and become nearly hypnotic. Soon, you are outside yourself and dwelling in exquisite beauty.

The 6th movement is a journey from this world to another, capable of piercing your heart.

We know that the great musicians of the day recognized Mozart's genius, among them Salieri, who was a respected musician at that time.

Many of them resented Mozart's music and resisted it.

Why?

Because his music threatened their reputations, their positions, and their musical scope. They may have recognized its transcendent qualities. However, other composers, like Franz Joseph Haydn, were not threatened by Mozart and therefore could fully appreciate it.

A Word about Performers

It's easy to be critical of performances. We all have our preferences and tastes. But sometimes it's worthwhile to remember that where we put our attention may make all of the difference.

In the 1960s, a great Russian cellist named Gregor Piatigorsky published his autobiography, simply titled *Cellist*. He always wanted to meet Pablo Casals, the legendary cellist. One day he was invited to the home of a wealthy family to play for a guest who wanted to hear him.

His story of meeting Pablo Casals reminds us how the truly legendary musical masters approach music.

> I was introduced to a little bald man with a pipe. He said that he was pleased to meet young musicians such as Serkin and me. Rudolf Serkin, who stood stiffly next to me, seemed, like myself, to be fighting his diffidence.

> Rudi had played before my arrival, and Casals now wanted to hear us together. Beethoven's *D-Major Sonata* was on the piano. "Why don't you play it?" asked Casals. Both nervous and barely knowing each other, we gave a poor performance that terminated somewhere in the middle.

"Bravo! Bravo! Wonderful!" Casals applauded.
Francesco brought the Schumann *Cello Concerto*,
which Casals wanted to hear. I never played worse.
Casals asked for Bach. Exasperated, I obliged with a
performance matching the Beethoven and
Schumann.

"Splendid! Magnifique!" said Casals, embracing me.

Gregor left the house confused because he knew he had
played badly. Why did the great master Casals praise him so
strongly? This behavior struck Gregor as insincere and caused
him great pain. A few years later he met Casals in Paris and
discovered to his great shame and delight that Casals was doing
something quite different.

We had dinner together and played duets for two
cellos, and I played for him until late at night.
Spurred by his great warmth, and happy, I confessed
what I had thought of his praising me in Berlin.

He reacted with sudden anger. He rushed to the
cello, "Listen!" He played a phrase from the
Beethoven sonata. "Didn't you play this fingering?
Ah, you did! It was novel to me...it was good...and
hcre, didn't you attack that passage with up-bow,
like this?" he demonstrated. He went through
Schumann and Bach, always emphasizing all he liked
that I had done.

"And for the rest," he said passionately, "leave it to
the ignorant and stupid who judge by counting only
the faults. I can be grateful, and so must you be, for
even one note, one wonderful phrase." I left with the

feeling of having been with a great artist and a friend.

I recall hearing a story of a student who had attended one of Pablo Casals' Master Classes for cello. The student told of how near the beginning of the class Casals played a single note on the cello.

The student revealed that somehow that single note transported him into a musical realm that completely changed his life. As a performing master, Casals brought everything in him to a single note, just as Mozart brought everything to every note and the whole piece he was composing.

Every note matters, and every note contributes to the wholeness of the entire piece.

Here is Pablo Casals in 1954, age 77, playing the most famous of cello solos, by Johann Sebastian Bach. The audio and video are old, but masters are masters, and somehow they rise above recording technologies of the time:

Video 4: Bach: *Suite for Unaccompanied Cello, No. 1*

In the next chapter, we will look as Mozart's childhood and his family so that we can explode some myths and get closer to how a composer like Mozart comes to be.

And we look at some of his amazing youthful works.

Chapter 3

Mozart—The Child, the Myth, the Man

"Listening to Mozart, we cannot think of any possible improvement...
21 piano sonatas, 27 piano concertos, 41 symphonies, 18 masses, 13
operas, 9 oratorios and cantata, 2 ballets, 40 plus concertos for
various instruments, string quartets, trios and quintets, violin and
piano duets, piano quartets, and the songs. This astounding output
includes hardly one work less than a masterpiece."
George Szell, Hungarian conductor

Playlist 3: MarkAndreAlexander.com/One-Click-to-Mozart/
(16 videos, 6 hrs. 20 min)

How do we account for Mozart's amazing skills as a composer
and performer?

Perhaps if Johann Sebastian Bach were reborn as Mozart, we could explain Mozart's amazing skills at such an early age.

Johannes Chrysostomus Wolfgangus Theophilus Mozart was born January 27, 1756. (He signed some letters in Latin as "Wolfgangus Amadeus Mozartus," but as a playful joke.)

What happened next is stunning:

- At age 3, he is drawn to his sister's clavier (an early piano) and starts spending endless hours playing. His father, Leopold, a professional court composer, musician, and music teacher, begins giving him instruction.

- At 4, he demonstrates his ability to learn a minuet and trio in thirty minutes. His father realizes he has a son unlike other children. Mozart writes his first composition (calling it a "concerto"), and invents his own system of musical notation.

- At 5, he writes his first compositions that survive (K. 1a, 1b, 1c, 1d, 1e, and 1f). He begins learning Latin. His father takes him to Munich, Germany, for three weeks to play for music lovers, including the elector of Bavaria, Maximilian III Joseph.

His very first surviving composition, nineteen seconds short and not fully formed, is remarkable in how it changes meter in the middle of the piece:

Video 1: K. 1a: *Andante in C*

This one, however, is perfectly formed:

Video 2: K. 1e: *Minuet in G* (scrolling score)

- At 6, he teaches himself to play violin, and performs second violin in a trio rehearsal in his home. He displays speed and accuracy, and an uncanny sense of time. People give him a musical idea for a fugue, and he improvises variations on it for hours.

To get a quick understanding of *theme and variations*, listen to this well-known Mozart tune that we know as "Twinkle Twinkle Little Star":

Video 3: K. 265: *12 Variations on "Ah, vous dirai-je, Maman" in C*

His father takes him to Vienna, Austria, for three months, amazing the court of Archduke Joseph, later Emperor Joseph II. Mozart calls for the court composer Wegenseil and plays one of Wegenseil's concertos while having the composer turn the pages.

The following keyboard piece reflects Mozart's delight and playful approach to composition:

Video 4: K. 5: *Minuet in F*

- At 7, he begins a three-year performance tour of Europe. His family is the guest of royal families, high nobility, and the cream of society.

He demonstrates his ability to sight-read at the keyboard or violin anything composed by others up to that time.

He begins learning French and Italian, in which he eventually becomes fluent.

Here is a typical announcement, for a London performance:

*"Miss Mozart of eleven and Master Mozart
of seven Years of Age, Prodigies of Nature;
taking the opportunity of representing to
the Public the greatest Prodigy that Europe
or that Human Nature has to boast of.
Every Body will be astonished to hear a Child
of such tender Age playing the Harpsichord
in such a Perfection—it surmounts all
Fantastic and Imagination* [sic], *and it is
hard to express which is more astonishing,
his Execution upon the Harpsichord playing
at Sight, or his own Composition."*

Mozart writes his first violin sonata (for violin and keyboard). His compositional complexity is developing rapidly:

Video 5: K. 6: *Violin Sonata in C*

- At 8, he dedicates six Sonatas he composes for Harpsichord, Violin, and Cello to England's Queen Charlotte, wife of King George III (K. 10-15).

He sits on the lap of Johann Christian Bach (one of the famous composer's many sons), and they improvise alternately on the same keyboard before the King and Queen for two hours.

He writes his first three-movement (K. 16):

Video 6: K. 16: *Symphony No. 1 in E-flat*

- At 9, he becomes the family's main source of income. He composes more symphonies, arias, and a keyboard sonata for four hands (K. 19d):

Video 7: K. 19: *Symphony No. 4 in D*

- At 10, he plays violin up to concert standard, knows all the orchestral instruments, and is able to talk to performers in their specialized language. He also composes in Paris his first religious work, the 4-minute *Kyrie in F*:

    Video 8: K. 33: *Kyrie in F*

- At 11, he writes his first piano concerto (K. 37) and his first cantata *Grabmusik* (K. 42):

    Video 9: K. 37: *Piano Concerto No. 1 in F*
    Video 10: K. 42: *Grabmusik*

    He also composes his first opera, *Apollo et Hyacinthus* (K. 38), a Latin musical comedy:

    Video 11: K. 38: *Apollo et Hyacinthus*

    He's able to collaborate with other professionals, like Michael Haydn, the brother of the famous composer Franz Joseph Haydn.

- At 12, he contracts smallpox, limiting his musical output to eleven pieces that still is enough music to fill several CDs, including another opera, three symphonies, and three religious masses:

    Video 12: K. 49: *Missa brevis in G*

- At 13, he writes another opera while in Vienna, several symphonies, two religious masses, and three cassations designed as light outdoor chamber performances.

    This simple and beautiful 27-minute Cassation for small chamber orchestra is in eight movements:

Video 13: K. 62a/100: *Cassation in D*

- At 14, he has his first operatic hit, *Mitridate, rè di Ponto* (Mitridate, King of Pontus), written for the city of Milan, Italy (this work is three hours long):

Video 14: K. 87: *Mitridate, rè di Ponto*

In his excellent course for The Teaching Company, "Great Masters: Mozart—His Life and Music," Professor Robert Greenberg outlines more of Mozart's incredible skills:

> "His ability to remember the most complex music after only a single hearing and to later write it down note perfect. His ability to improvise better than others could compose. His ability to compose entire symphonies and concerti in his head, and then write out the individual instrumental parts without having to first write out the score."

So in the face of all of these incredible skills, exhibited at such an early age, the question arises:

How do people,
especially "experts" of past and present times,
explain Mozart?

1. *Satanic witchcraft:* At a performance in Naples, one observer claimed Mozart wore a magic ring to aid his impossibly dexterous left hand. He sold his soul, trading a long life for great music.

2. *A creature of God:* Divine music could not be created by a man, but someone all or partially divine.

3. *A musical monster:* Created by his father, Leopold.

4. *A transmigrated soul:* He reincarnated into this life already skilled.

5. *A genetic freak of nature:* The man-child who cannot help what he is, and never became a real adult, as seen in the film *Amadeus.*

Whatever the case, Mozart was *not* the man-child depicted in *Amadeus.*

> *His later actions reveal an accomplished adult*
> *in social, financial, and political life.*

That's not to say he didn't gamble or face debts, or act politically incorrect to preserve the integrity of his music. Mozart's temperament was that of a genius and artist, but not at the expense of being an adult.

Then why has the man-child myth endured?

When looking at a Mozart (or a Shakespeare or a Van Gogh), we may find it difficult to believe they are human like the rest of us. So we look for excuses to dehumanize them, making them either less than or more than human. Automatons or demigods.

> *Mozart had amazing talent, but he worked*
> *extraordinarily hard to manifest that talent.*

As a child he was known to compose every morning from 6:00 to 9:00 A.M. and play the clavier and compose music from 8:00 P.M. to midnight. In the middle of the day he would compose if he had to write something quickly.

He was curious to learn about everything: drawing, reading, writing, arithmetic, history, geography, and foreign languages.

But his bias was music. And his father took advantage of that interest, supposedly for the good of the family, but more for the good of himself. Although Mozart's mother and sister played a peripheral role in Mozart's life, Mozart's father served as a key character in Mozart's development and early experience.

Mozart's Family

Mozart's mother, Anna Maria Mozart, died while she and Mozart were traveling. Mozart was 22. She seemed to prefer being in the background, so little is known about her. She married Leopold Mozart in 1747 in Salzburg. Although they had seven children, only two survived.

Mozart's sister, Anna Maria Walburga Ignatia, was born 1751 and nicknamed "Nannerl" as a child. She died seventy-eight years later.

Mozart's father was a composer and violinist, but did not have the musical success he wanted. So he lived it through his son. Leopold did not have his son's skill, but he did have musical taste.

Here is Leopold's *Trumpet Concerto in D*. Listen to it for a minute or two to get a sense of Mozart's father's rather mediocre but pleasant style. Mozart's youthful compositions tower over his father's compositions:

Video 15: Leopold Mozart: *Trumpet Concerto in D*

Leopold held authority in contempt, and therefore was a difficult man leading a difficult life. But he was driven. And seeing his son's talent, he did all he could to help his son blossom, perform, *and make money.*

And perhaps just as importantly, he used his son for revenge—revenge against his own mother, who gave all of her children a dowry, except Leopold.

When Mozart was nearly two years old, Leopold was appointed court composer by the Salzburg prince-archbishop. Over the next few years, he had plenty of opportunity to show off his son. But Salzburg at that time had only limited public exposure. By the time Mozart was five, Leopold set his sights elsewhere.

He first arranged a three-week concert tour in Munich in 1761. In 1762, he arranged a three-month tour in Vienna, performances that started the child Mozart's rise to fame and fortune. Apparently, Leopold did not do any more composition after this year.

In 1763, as if everything comes in threes, Leopold initiated the famous three-year concert tour of Europe. Mozart performed in eighty-eight cities across Europe. They spent fifteen of those months in London due to the incredibly positive reception given to the young 7-year-old Mozart.

This tour would have been dismissed as myth had not so many people in so many cities documented what they saw.

> The famous writer of *Faust*, Johann Wolfgang von Goethe (1749-1832), saw the 7-year-old Mozart perform in Frankfurt in 1763. He vividly recalled the "little man with his wig and his sword."

> Goethe lamented that Mozart never set his *Faust* to music. However, in 1775 he did write a singspiel text, *Erwin und Elmire*, containing a German song that Mozart set to music ten years later.

Video 16: K. 476: *Das Veilchen*

Leopold appears to have been Mozart's only formal teacher. However, while touring and performing, Mozart received the direct and indirect tutelage of Europe's foremost musical composers. The foremost was Johann Christian Bach, whom he met in London.

The Mozart children (Marianne, nicknamed Nannerl, performed with him, but young Mozart stole all the press) received gifts and money wherever they performed.

And Leopold was right there
accepting the expensive gifts
and counting the gold and silver coins.

By the end of that tour, young Mozart became the primary financial foundation for his family. But Mozart never received the royal appointment that he richly deserved.

And Leopold, basing his dependence on his son, did all he could to keep Mozart with the family. Leopold later objected to Mozart marrying at a time when Mozart stood ready to leave the nest completely.

But Mozart left both his Salzburg home and his father. They wrote little to each other.

His father, a man of dearly held resentments, never recovered from Mozart making his claim of adulthood. He died an unhappy man, about four years prior to his son's death.

Mozart, meanwhile, had his best years before him.

Next, we again listen closely to a single work, in this case the overture to the opera *The Magic Flute.* Our focus this time is on *musical architecture.* The more you understand some musical architecture, the more jewels you will hear in Mozart's music.

Chapter 4

Hearing Mozart, Part 2:
The Magic Flute, Overture

*"Does it not seem as if Mozart's works become
fresher and fresher the oftener we hear them?"*
Robert Schumann

Playlist 4: MarkAndreAlexander.com/One-Click-to-Mozart/
(4 videos, 26 min)

Mozart wrote stellar musical architecture.

For the modern listener of popular music, listening to
Mozart requires a new kind of listening, an architectural space-
time way of listening, as revolutionary to young modern ears as
Einstein's theory of relativity was to early 20th-century scientific
minds.

Some of that architecture has to do with the "classical style" of composing, or more specifically, the Viennese classical style, since the city of Vienna, Austria, served as its home.

Mozart took the classical style to its apex.

While it's not the purpose of this book to go deep into compositional theory, a few things are worth noting about the classical style. (We will introduce a bit more on compositional structure in the next chapter.)

The three great composers in the classical style are Haydn, Mozart, and Beethoven. Haydn significantly developed the style, Mozart took it to its apex, and Beethoven established its breadth and power as a basis for the coming Romantic Style.

Haydn was 24 years old when Mozart was born, and he lived eighteen years after Mozart's death, carrying on the tradition and passing it to young Beethoven.

The young Beethoven arrived in Vienna in 1792 with an album given to him by his patron, Count Waldstein.

In it, Waldstein had written: "You are going to Vienna in fulfillment of your long frustrated wishes... You will receive the spirit of Mozart from the hands of Haydn."

Beethoven's desire to study with Mozart died with Mozart's passing in 1791. But as its name suggests, the classical style connects back to the classical time of ancient Greece and Rome. Enlightenment thinkers and artists loved the clarity of intent, the clean lines, and the overall unity and harmony especially dominant in fifth-century Greek culture.

The ultimate embodiment of the ancient
classical style is in the Parthenon.

The Parthenon represents an enduring symbol of, not only Ancient Greece and Athenian democracy, but also western civilization.

English historian John Cooper calls it "the most perfect Doric temple ever built. Even in antiquity, its architectural refinements were legendary, especially the subtle correspondence between the curvature of the [platform of three steps], the taper of the [inner chamber] walls and the [changing diameter] of the columns."

The architecture embodied the height of clarity and apparent simplicity, characteristics later taken up during the Enlightenment.

The Enlightenment era, from the 1620s to the 1780s, embodied a new kind of humanism, similar to that of the ancient Greeks. Up until then, the role of the church and group singing in Europe played a huge role in music. The musical focus tended to be strongly toward the religiously divine and the music was highly ornamented and complex.

The Enlightenment shift into a new subjective view of music reflected the shift to individual humans, resulting in greater individual vocal lyricism and a greater clarity and simplicity in the music.

The classical style of Haydn and Mozart was a break from the highly ornamented and cyclical baroque style of Vivaldi and Bach. This new style moved toward the more narrative and linear, celebrating several key characteristics:

1. Melodic beauty.

2. Melodic clarity.

3. Like the Parthenon, a kind of formal purity and balance.

4. Good taste, meaning a kind of expressive restraint (which begins loosening with Beethoven).

The creation of new instruments with more dynamic range partially accounts for and supports this change.

For example, let's look at the evolution from the harpsichord to the fortepiano or simply piano. (In Italian, *forte* means "loud" and *piano* means "soft.")

Conductor Thomas Beecham was alleged to have said,

> *"The sound of a harpsichord is like two skeletons copulating on a tin roof."*

The harpsichord displayed a tinny, limited dynamic range. It could not play very loudly, which is why it is often drowned out when used in a modern orchestra. It could hold its own only in a small chamber environment.

The piano carried a greater richness and depth of tone, with its ability to respond to a light or heavy touch. The piano provided more dynamic range to enhance melodic beauty and clarity.

Here are famous pieces of Bach's music played first on harpsichord and then on the piano. Bach did not compose for the piano, since it did not yet exist, but this comparison demonstrates the difference the choice of instrument makes.

Video 1: Bach: *Goldberg Variations, Aria* (Cooper, harpsichord)

Video 2: Bach: *Goldberg Variations, Aria* (Barenboim, piano)

In the baroque style, instruments without a great dynamic range were suited for the cyclical, group-oriented presentation of music that embodies so much religious music of those times. The audience expected a dynamic range only slightly louder or softer.

In the classical style, instruments allowed for greater *individual* expression through pure and balanced forms. Individual expression would be viewed as a form of heresy during the Baroque period.

Furthermore, the additional dynamic range in newer instruments allows a composer to extend and even invent new musical architectures.

Mozart took advantage of the new fortepiano's capabilities and provided us with some of the first dramatic piano concertos. (See Chapter 5.)

Another key to classical style was this move from high ornamentation, as is evident in almost all of Bach's works, to a style with cleaner lines and sharper, almost jewel-like reflections.

What do I mean by jewel-like reflections?

Let's listen to the opening minutes of the overture to *The Magic Flute* (*Die Zauberflöte*). You will hear musical development rather than musical *ornamentation*. Stop at 03:11 when the music hits its first break

Video 3: *K. 620: The Magic Flute (Overture)*

Here's how the opening 02:05 minutes break down. Listen again so you can understand what you are hearing. The key passage starts at 01:29 and ends seconds later.

We will focus on those four seconds.

00:01-01:13: Gentle opening.

01:14: The second violins start with the main melodic theme.

01:29: The first violins start with the main theme, but at a higher pitch. The first and second violins play off of each other until...

01:37: The cellos start with the main theme, while the violins playfully move around them. And then comes the start of something few hear the first time:

01:46: As the violins come back with the main theme, the underlying basses launch an octave followed by falling notes.

This launch and fall is like fireworks being launched into the sky and falling *two seconds in advance of* the violins doing the same fireworks-like launch and fall at 01:48.

Listen over and over again until you hear it.

*What you are hearing is a spatial
and temporal reflection of a musical phrase.*

Most people expect to hear reflections of a main theme
after it is played. But before?

Think of Beethoven's famous four-note theme that starts
his *Symphony No. 5 in C minor*:

> Da-Da-Da-Duhhhhhhh... Da-Da-Da-
> Duhhhhhhh...
>
> Da-Da-Da-Duh, Da-Da-Da-Duh, Da-Da-Da-
> Duhhhhhhh...

And so on...

But Mozart subtlety slips in this one *before* the main melody
arrives there. Just like fireworks announcing the arrival of the
main segment of the overture.

This is a tiny example of Mozart's great art. Simple, elegant,
clean, and expressively powerful, and often hidden if the listener
is not actively *listening*.

And this tiny example is suggestive of what's to come.

Once you begin to listen closely to this overture, looking for
reflections, you hear a rich tapestry of instruments playing with
themes and variations.

In fact, if you go back to the first minute, and listen to the
basses, you will hear this same kind of advance announcement of
a musical phrase several times.

It's Mozart's way of telling you that the hidden is there before the reality. This plays into some of the Masonic symbolism imbued throughout the opera.

As you come to know the entire overture, you can turn it in your mind's ear like a diamond, noting the stunning beauty of its many reflections and refractions, both in space and time.

> *It's as if the entire overture arrived whole*
> *in Mozart's consciousness, and he was*
> *merely transcribing the whole within*
> *the constraints of space and time.*

But that's only the beginning.

There's an entire *three-hour* opera here that the overture is announcing. So much of the overture gets reflected throughout the opera: the story, the songs, the characters, the drama, the metaphors, the underlying meanings, the symbols...

Is it any wonder that people who love opera, *love opera*?

Like studying Shakespeare or Da Vinci or Plato, there is an endless variety of beauty to discover throughout one's lifetime.

No matter how long you live and study, great art manages to stay one step ahead of you. There is always something new to discover, something more to understand, something greater to experience, something more refined to become.

> *Great Art improves you*
> *the more you take it into your consciousness.*

In the next section, we drill down into Sonata form, which appears throughout so much classical music.

Extended Discussion

Structurally, the classical style of non-vocal music—like symphonies, concertos, and chamber music—most often exhibits "Sonata form." (Other forms include *theme and variations, minuet, trio,* and *rondo.*)

When a musical movement is structured according to sonata form, two or more themes are introduced, developed, and then returned to in their original order.

Sonata form reflects how an opera unfolds:

1. Introduction of characters.

2. Development of character and action with many interesting changes.

3. Some kind of reveal or *denouement.*

4. The finale.

In sonata form these are called:

1. *Exposition* (introduction of two or more contrasting themes in different musical keys).

2. *Development* (the themes are transformed, blended, and juxtaposed; this is where a virtuoso performer may show off).

3. *Recapitulation* (the themes return in their original order).

4. *Coda* (the musical finale, where a series of *cadences* complete the movement; cadences sound like short musical conclusions, a kind of *Ta-Da*).

Sonata form—as a reflection of 18th century enlightenment attitudes—aimed for thematic and structural clarity and purity and expressive restraint. (Some of that restraint gave way during Beethoven's lifetime after 1805; in some sense, the classical style ended after Beethoven's *Symphony No. 3 in E-flat*.)

Let's listen to the entire seven-minute overture to *The Magic Flute* paying particular attention to the sonata form in the first few minutes.

Video 3: *K. 620: The Magic Flute (Overture)*

Introduction: 00:01 - 01:13 (the opening presents the three rising pitches of the "tonic chord," E-flat, G, and B-flat; the idea of threes reappears throughout the music; tonic refers to the note, in this case E-flat, around which the entire musical scale is formed).

Exposition: 01:14 - 03:10 (multiple main themes are introduced).

Development: 03:11 - 04:56 (notice all the beautiful falling phrases across the instruments at 03:58, and then at 04:05 the section where the double basses and cellos anticipate the melody).

Recapitulation: 04:56 - 05:59 (we have a sense of coming home to the music we first heard in the exposition, even though it is not a precise repeat).

Coda: 06:06 - 06:40 (you can feel the finale building, and then comes around to the tonic pitches once again; Mozart collapses the three pitches and ends with three solid, final E-flats).

The way the overture begins (three rising tonic pitches) and ends (a grand re-enactment of the opening three rising pitches followed by the final three E-flats) demonstrates the formal architectural beauty in the classical style and Mozart's realization of it.

Musicians, Mathematics, and Symbols

Much has been written about Mozart, Masonry, and symbolism. Masonry refers to "freemasonry," a kind of guild originally formed by stonemasons, but later becoming a kind of members-only society interested in mathematics, brotherhood, and architectural symbols.

Composers often played with the mathematics of their music.

Bach, for example, like many of his contemporaries, believed numbers were divine, and he used the symbolic ideas of numbers throughout his works.

He frequently embodied cryptographically his own name in a theme: B-A-C-H:

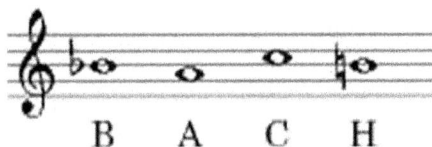

B = B-flat and the number 2

A = A and the number 1

C = C and the number 3

H = B natural and the number 8

2+1+3+8=14 (Apparently, 14, and its mirror 41, were among Bach's favorite numbers. These numbers appear to be hidden many times within Bach's musical structure.)

The most famous example of Bach's name used in his music is in the *Canonic variations on 'Vom Himeel hoch.'* It's found in the very last measure:

Video 4: Bach: *Canonic variations on "Vom Himeel hoch"*

Classical composers saw moods, emotions, or subjective qualities associated with different keys.

For example, the key of G minor would express sadness and tragedy, while the key of B minor would express a quiet acceptance of fate and gentle compliance. G major on the other hand was considered the "key of benediction." Beethoven regarded A-flat major as the primary key for his slow movements.

In 1806, Christian Schubart compiled a list of the characteristics of musical keys, at least as perceived at that time:

> *C major:* Completely pure; innocence, simplicity, naivety, childlike.

> *C minor:* Declaring love and lamenting unhappy love; languishing, longing, sighing of the love-sick soul.

> *Db major:* Degenerating into grief and rapture; cannot laugh, but can smile; cannot howl, but can grimace; for unusual characters and feelings.

> *D major:* Triumph, war cries, victor, and rejoicing; for

symphonies, marches, holiday songs, heavenly choruses.

D minor: Melancholy womanliness, anger and brooding.

D# minor: Soul's deep distress, brooding despair, blackest depression; every fear of a shuddering.

Eb major: Love, of devotion, an intimate conversation with God.

E major: Shouts of joy, laughing pleasure, full delight.

F major: Complaisance and calm.

F minor: Deep depression, funereal lament, groans of misery, longing for death.

F# major: Triumph over difficulty, the sigh of relief after surmounting great obstacles; echo of the struggling and then conquering soul.

F# minor: Gloom, resentment, and discontent.

G major: Rustic, idyllic, lyrical; every satisfied passion, every tender gratitude for true friendship and faithful love, every gentle and peaceful emotion of the heart.

G minor: Discontent, uneasiness, worry about failures; gnashing of teeth, resentment, and dislike.

Ab major: Death, the grave, judgment, eternity.

Ab minor: Grumbling, suffocating heart being squeezed, wailing lament, difficult struggle.

A major: Declarations of innocent love, hope of seeing one's beloved again, youthful cheerfulness, trust in God.

A minor: Pious womanliness, tenderness.

Bb major: Cheerful love, clear conscience, hope for a better world.

Bb minor: Surliness, unpleasant countenance; mocking God and the world; discontent with everything; preparation for suicide.

B major: Wild passions; anger, rage, jealousy, fury, despair, all burdens of the heart.

B minor: Patience, the calm that awaits one's fate, submission to divine dispensation.

Whatever Mozart's intentions regarding Masonic, mathematical symbolism, or musical moods, *The Magic Flute* stands as a testament to how Mozart can offer people of different interests ways of exploring deeply different aspects of music.

Although *The Magic Flute* was not Mozart's last composition, some think it qualifies as his last definitive work, the capstone of his unique gifts. According to musicologist Alfred Einstein:

> "It was his bequest to mankind, his appeal to the ideals of humanity. His last work is not *[La Clemenza di] Tito* or the *Requiem*; it is *Die Zauberflöte.* Into the Overture...he compressed the struggle and victory of mankind, using the symbolic means of polyphony [two or more simultaneous lines of independent melody]; working out, laboriously working out in the development section; struggle and triumph."

Chapter 5

Mozart's Piano Concertos

"The 'Jeunehomme' piano concerto [No. 9] is Mozart's first great masterpiece. He was twenty-one when he composed it.... Although he had already written many astonishing things which prepared the way for his later mastery, it is with the "Jeunehomme" concerto that this mastery begins..."
Alfred Brendel, pianist

Playlist 5: MarkAndreAlexander.com/One-Click-to-Mozart/
(28 videos, 9 hrs 53 min)

Mozart had an orchestral mind.

In his early piano sonatas (solo piano pieces), Mozart composed with an eye towards themes and variations, minuets and trios, rondos, and marches.

Mozart's later piano sonatas sound more complex, but they always maintain a kind of singing quality. In other words, Mozart heard his melodies as singing voices and often composed as if those melodic lines were to be sung.

These sonatas are wonderful in themselves, but when we think of the great piano sonatas, we typically turn to Beethoven.

Why?

Even when Mozart composed for piano as a single instrument, he could not help but compose as if for a singer and an orchestra. The key to listening to his piano sonatas, especially his later ones, is to listen as if to an opera or a symphony.

Beethoven, on the other hand, came to the piano on its own terms and composed accordingly, or more precisely, for his ideal of a piano, which would not be fully realized until later in the 19th century. The piano in Beethoven's day had started to develop into a much more powerful solo musical instrument.

In his piano sonatas, Beethoven attempts to wring the maximum music possible from the piano. In Beethoven's hands, the music displays individual expression. In Beethoven's sonatas, the orchestral angle we find in Mozart is not nearly as evident.

Let's quickly compare Mozart's final piano sonata to Beethoven's.

Video 1: K. 576: Mozart's *Piano Sonata in D* (Uchida)

Video 2: Beethoven: *Piano Sonata, No. 32, Opus 111* (Barenboim)

It is ironic, then, that the place where Mozart releases his greatest individual and expressionistic piano playing is in his piano concertos.

Alfred Brendel, a concert pianist and one of the great interpreters of Mozart, said in an online 2002 interview:

> Mozart is one of the most sensuous composers ever. There is a sensuality too about his melodies. I'm reminded of a lovely sentence from [Ferruccio] Busoni, who said ... there was no doubt that Mozart took singing as his starting point, and from this stems the uninterrupted melodiousness which shimmers through his compositions like the lovely forms of a woman through the folds of a flimsy dress.

> Isn't that wonderful?

> And with Mozart, of course, you also have the quite amazing expressiveness which goes beyond what Busoni...would concede: Mozart's art of characterization from an early age was bound up with his observation of human beings.

> Mozart clearly observed people continually, and as a child took delight in improvising human emotions and reactions in the form of arias.

The concerto is an Enlightenment idea, an intellectual movement of the late 17th and 18th centuries that emphasized reason and individualism over tradition. The Enlightenment moved away from tribal "group-think" and began emphasizing the *individual* without venturing into overly dramatic self-expression as happened during the Romantic era.

Although it germinated in the Baroque era and flowered with Vivaldi and Bach, the concerto's full expression arrived with Mozart.

A Mozart concerto pits an individual instrument against the orchestra.
They play on an equal footing.

In a violin concerto, one violinist holds the stage equally with the orchestra. In a flute concerto, one flautist holds the stage equally with the orchestra. And with a piano concerto, one pianist holds the stage equally with the orchestra.

The concerto is, at its core, theater—a kind of conversation. The soloist proclaims his or her strength to challenge and then harmonize with the entire orchestra, like an opera soprano taking center stage for a solo *aria*, next performing as part of a duet, and then finally as part of a full chorus.

The concerto offers the soloist the greatest range of musical expression, brought to its heights by Mozart.

Many regard Mozart's piano concertos to be his greatest orchestral compositions.

Later musical theorists love to analyze Mozart's concertos and establish musical boundaries and limits about how one would compose a Mozartian concerto. But you should understand that Mozart would likely have laughed at the idea.

He would more likely say to later composers, "Be yourself. Invent, play, perform. Strike out and be new, with taste."

There is an exhibitionist streak in Mozart with his concertos.

For Mozart, a concerto is written for the composer as performer. They are linked. He would say to any performer of his concertos, "Make these your own."

He would understand what Chopin meant when he wrote:

> "I am writing without knowing what my pen is scribbling, because at this moment Liszt is playing my etudes and transporting me outside of my respectable thoughts. I should like to steal from him the way he plays my own etudes."

A Note about Tempo

Classical music relies on Italian descriptions of how fast the music is played. This list of the more common terms starts from the slowest to the fastest, includes an approximate number of beats per minute (BPM) to convey the relative speeds.

Notice the fastest is about 10 times faster than the slowest.

Larghissimo – very, very slow (20 BPM)

Grave – very slow (30 BPM)

Largo – broadly (40 BPM)

Lento – slowly (50 BPM)

Larghetto – rather broadly (60 BPM)

Adagio – slow and stately (70 BPM)

Andante – at a walking pace (85 BPM)

Andante moderato – between andante and moderato (95 BPM)

Moderato – moderately (110 BPM)

Allegretto – moderately fast (115 BPM)

Allegro moderato – closer to allegro (120 BPM)

Allegro – fast, quickly, and bright (140 BPM)

Allegro assai – between allegro and vivace (155 BPM)

Vivace – lively and fast (170 BPM)

Allegro vivace – very fast (175 BPM)

Presto – extremely fast (180 BPM)

Prestissimo – even faster than Presto (200 BPM)

Piano Concerto No. 9 in E-flat, "Jeunehomme"

Let's start with what Alfred Brendel calls "Mozart's first great masterpiece," written in Salzburg around his 21st birthday. Listen to the 1st movement *allegro*:

Video 3: K. 271: *Piano Concerto No. 9 in E-flat* (I. Allegro, Brendel)

In this fully mature work, Mozart appears to be composing beyond his years. The piano engages with the orchestra as an equal, something we don't see until his next fully mature piano concerto seven years later, No. 17 in G major (K. 453).

(This does not mean that the concertos in between aren't great. They are. But the *Jeunehomme* was years ahead of its time.)

Unlike any of his other piano concertos, the piano interrupts the orchestra almost from the beginning. Mozart has the piano enter into a delightful dialog with the orchestra. Later, the orchestra interrupts the piano, as if it were paying back the compliment.

The piano and orchestra share a musical intimacy within constantly changing musical patterns on the main theme throughout both the development and recapitulation. (See Chapter 4.)

The 2nd movement *andantino* is uncharacteristic of most of Mozart's 2nd movements. This one is slow, almost despondent in its theme.

Video 4: K. 271: *Piano Concerto No. 9 in E-flat* (II. Andante, Anda)

The 2nd movement seems to anticipate the 3rd movement *presto* by creating a black velvet background for the diamond-like charm that closes out the concerto. (A diamond displays more brilliantly on black.)

The contrast sharpens the beauty and delight of both the 1st and 3rd movements.

Video 5: K. 271: *Piano Concerto No. 9 in E-flat* (III. Presto, Anda)

Notice how, in the middle of the 3rd movement, he strikes out in a different key with a completely different emotional feeling—a minuet that, in effect, places a movement within a movement.

> *This is the kind of piano playing that influenced Frederic Chopin so greatly.*

Listen to the slow part starting at 03.49.

Then listen to this nocturne by Chopin:

Video 6: Chopin: *Nocturne in E-flat, Op. 9, No. 2*

Now listen to the complete piano concerto performed by Mitsuko Uchida. Mozart is always a delight in her hands.

Video 7: K. 271: *Piano Concerto No. 9 in E-flat* (complete, Uchida)

Piano Concerto No. 12 in A

Although not considered one of Mozart's twelve mature piano concertos (9, 17-27), this is one of my all-time favorites.

Johann Christian Bach, one of Mozart's favorite teachers while in England, taught him how to write concertos. He died in 1782, shortly before Mozart wrote this piano concerto.

The 2nd movement is based on a melody by J.C. Bach, and is one of the most beautiful 2nd movements by Mozart. We should all be so fortunate to be remembered by such a lovely piece of music.

Video 8: K. 414: *Piano Concerto No. 12 in A* (II. Andante, Pollini)

Here's the complete concerto. The more I listen to it, the more my heart opens:

Video 9: K. 414: *Piano Concerto No. 12 in A* (complete, Uchida)

Piano Concerto No. 17 in G

Mozart wrote piano concertos for his own performances. He would advertise subscription concerts featuring himself as the piano soloist in his concertos. He imbued an incredible sense of play, variety, and compositional mastery in his piano concertos.

Mozart learned from J. C. Bach one musical form that he used the rest of his life—double exposition form. Double exposition simply means that Mozart introduces two separately composed themes in the opening exposition of the movement.

In the 1st movement *allegro*, the orchestra plays the first theme and the piano introduces a second. Mozart develops the second theme. Notice how the melodies start out simple and then Mozart begins weaving them into a creative texture.

In the 2nd movement *andante*, starting at 11:45, Mozart displays the height of *orchestral color.*

> *Orchestral color is another name for* timbre.

Imagine the same note played on a guitar, then a violin, and finally on a flute. The difference among the three is timbre, the *color* of the note.

Orchestral color, then, refers to different instruments taking turns playing a theme and providing development or variations on that theme. The hearer enjoys the abundant color of the instruments.

The 3rd movement *allegretto* presents a theme with variations full of the joy, the hallmark of Mozart's delight in composition.

Here is a complete performance of *Piano Concerto No. 17 in G* by Mitsuko Uchida, one of the finest performances available.

Video 10: K. 453: *Piano Concerto No. 17 in G* (complete, Uchida)

Piano Concerto No. 20 in D minor

Mozart's *Piano Concerto No. 20 in D minor* starts off darkly, at first, as if someone were anxiously on the run. The 1st movement *allegro* has moments of sunshine and calmness, but the anxiety never completely leaves us. This is a long movement, taking up nearly half the total time of the concerto.

The 2nd movement *romance* starts at 15:42 and provides a relaxed contrast to the 1st movement. Melodies pass back and forth in conversation between the piano and orchestra.

The 3rd movement *allegro assai* turns darkly again at 24:40 beginning with a mad rush, then alternates dark and light, powerful and fun, all the way to the end.

Video 11: K. 466: *Piano Concerto No. 20 in D minor* (complete, Uchida)

If you want to grasp the difference between Mozart and Beethoven, listen to the version below of the 1st movement with a *cadenza* written by Beethoven, and then to one by Mozart for his *Piano Concerto No. 27 in B-flat.*

A *cadenza* is an opportunity for the solo pianist to perform while the orchestra goes silent. The performer displays his or her virtuosity during the cadenza, which most often takes place near the end of the movement.

Often the composer will write the cadenza. However, sometimes the cadenza portion of the music is left blank for the pianist to invent. In some cases, performers will replace the composer's original cadenza with their own.

Beethoven wrote a cadenza for this piano concerto. Where Mozart's cadenzas are high elegance, Beethoven's are much more dramatic.

The performer of the Beethoven cadenza here is 12-year-old Billy Wu.

> **Video 12: K. 466: *Piano Concerto No. 27 in B-flat* (Mozart cadenza, Randalu)**

> **Video 13: K. 466: *Piano Concerto No. 20 in D minor* (Beethoven cadenza, Wu)**

Piano Concerto No. 21 in C

Mozart's most famous piano concerto is famous because the 1967 Swedish film *Elvira Madigan* used the 2nd movement as a theme. And for good reason!

But people often forget the rest of this magnificent concerto. Mozart displays complete confidence in its composition.

The 1st movement *allegro maestoso* (brisk and lively, but stately and majestically) has a long orchestral beginning. With repeated listenings, however, and by imagining Mozart as the performer, you can begin to see why.

The audience listens to the orchestra waiting for Master Mozart to begin. But they wait and wait, until finally Mozart starts in, as if saying, "Hey, whatever the orchestra can do, I can do better."

At first he repeats the orchestral theme in a virtuosic manner, but then introduces a second theme not heard before. Next he jumps into a series of *arpeggios* (scales and broken chords). These are not themes or even melodies as much as musical harmonies.

The 2nd movement *andante* (moderately slow) at 14:00 needs no explication. Just an ear that responds to the beautiful and the sublime. Except to note that the orchestra once again takes its time introducing the theme, leaving the audience to believe that nothing more beautiful can be constructed.

> *And yet, Mozart's piano arrives*
> *and takes the same theme*
> *into the heart of love.*

Mozart proves the validity of the newly invented *fortepiano* (later called the "piano.") And audiences as well as composers quickly forget that concertos used to be the domain of the harpsichord.

The 3rd movement *allegro vivace assai* (lively and fast) at 21:00 is quick and lively, showing off the virtuoso pianist.

This performance by the Murray Perahia shows how a well-conducted orchestra can form the perfect partner to pristine playing.

Mozart loved clarity and purity,
especially in piano playing.

You can hear every note by this piano master.

**Video 14: K. 467: *Piano Concerto No. 21 in C,*
(complete, Murray Perahia)**

Piano Concerto No. 23 in A

Where the *Piano Concerto No. 20 in D minor* has dark 1st and
3rd movements in a minor key, with a happy and fun major key
in the middle movement, the *Piano Concerto No. 23 in A* gives us
major keys surrounding a darker minor in the middle
movement.

And that 2nd movement *adagio*, starting at 11:22, though
bittersweet, is one of Mozart's most beautiful, simple, and heart-
directed.

Strangely, Mozart composes it in F-sharp minor, the only
time in all of Mozart's repertoire that he wrote a movement in
that key. You may recall that the mood for this key revolves
around gloom, resentment, and discontent, all uncharacteristic
of Mozart.

Listen to what he does with the woodwinds (clarinets, flutes,
and bassoons).

**Video 15: K. 488: *Piano Concerto No. 23 in A,*
(complete, Uchida)**

Piano Concertos No. 24, 25, 26, 27

Mozart's final four piano concertos are as great as the rest.

Both *Piano Concerto No. 24 in C minor* and *Piano Concerto
No. 25 in C* contain powerful musical ideas. *No. 25* especially
opens with triumph and majesty. And so it's ironic that his *Piano*

Concerto No. 26 in D is light and graceful, while being called "The Coronation" because he wrote it for the new Austrian emperor Leopold II.

His *Piano Concerto No. 27 in B-flat minor*, written in his final year, has been described as nostalgic, resigned, reflective, and rueful, peaceful, and a summing up.

All are worth a lifetime of listening:

> **Video 16: K. 491: *Piano Concerto No. 24 in C minor* (complete, Uchida)**
>
> **Video 17: K. 503: *Piano Concerto No. 25 in C* (complete, Uchida)**
>
> **Video 18: K. 537: *Piano Concerto No. 26 in D major* (The Coronation, complete, Uchida)**
>
> **Video 19: K. 595: *Piano Concerto No. 27 in B-flat* (complete, Uchida)**

If I were forced to choose among all the types of Mozart's musical compositions (symphony, piano concerto, opera, etc.) to take to that proverbial desert island, I would choose all of Mozart's piano concertos.

(The first four are actually arrangements by Leopold Mozart of music by other composers for a young Mozart to perform on his first tours.)

Perhaps I am biased because I am a pianist. Nevertheless, some of Mozart's most personal, orchestral, lyric, and gorgeous music can be found in these amazing works.

A lifetime of musical wonders here await you.

Other Kinds of Concertos

Mozart wrote only five violin concertos, but what masterpieces they are, especially the final three.

> *Mozart's violin concertos embody his childlike spirit of simple play and beauty.*

Here are performances by Itzhak Perlman on violin with James Levine conducting.

The exquisite 2nd movements in all three of these concertos will make you fall in love again with the violin. They purify the heart.

And if you are looking for music to make your heart soar, you want the 1st movement *allegro aperto* in the *Violin Concerto No. 5 in A major.* It's perfect.

Video 20: K. 216: *Violin Concerto No. 3 in G* (complete, Perlman)

Video 21: K. 218: *Violin Concerto No. 4 in D* (complete, Perlman)

Video 22: K. 219: *Violin Concerto No. 5 in A* (complete, Perlman)

Mozart did not like the flute. He found its timbre (color) too cold and hard, unlike the warmer clarinet and oboe. So we may never have had any flute music from Mozart had not a wealthy flute player commissioned several flute concertos and quartets.

> *Despite Mozart's bias against the flute, the music he composed for flute is exquisite.*

The *Flute Concerto No. 1 in G* is a perfect example of music to start your day or end your night.

You can practice viewing in more formal terms the double exposition of this concerto's themes in the 1st movement *allegro maestoso.* Here is how the themes break down in the first half of this 9-minute movement:

> 00:00: Theme 1 - Orchestral exposition
> 00:34: Theme 2 - Orchestral exposition
>
> 01:04: Theme 1 - Solo exposition
> 02:23: Theme 2 - Solo exposition (it returns at 6:20)
>
> 00:49 - 01:04 - Orchestral exposition of cadence material
> 02:40 - 03:31 - Solo exposition of cadence material
> (much expanded)
>
> 01:33 - 02:25 - Solo exposition (a third minor theme between themes 1 and 2)

> **Video 23: K. 313: *Flute Concerto No. 1 in G* (I. Allegro Maestoso, De Jean)**

Since music is so abstract (as opposed to spoken language), we sometimes forget that the composer communicates actual meaning through the musical forms, phrasings, melodies, and interplay of instruments.

The 1st movement demonstrates the contrast of double exposition form.

Listen to the first 3.5 minutes of the 1st movement straight through. The orchestra declares itself in a more bombastic way, as if a speaker were giving a rhetorical speech to the crowd.

On the other hand, the solo exposition is intimate, personal, more private. It's as if the speaker is having a conversation with us as an individual.

The double exposition form in music
contrasts the individual and the collective,
the public and the private,
the general and the personal.

Music can convey metaphorical meanings just like spoken language. We explore metaphor more explicitly in language and poetry in *Shakespeare and Great Literature: A Lifetime of Learning, Book 5* (to be published in 2016).

Mozart's Final Concerto

Mozart's final fully completed work, just a few weeks before his death in December 1791, was a clarinet concerto. He wrote it for a good friend, Anton Stadler, who at that time pioneered the use of a basset clarinet, which allowed a much deeper range.

Mozart wrote to Stadler, "Never would I have thought that the clarinet could be capable of imitating the human voice as deceptively as it is imitated by you. Truly your instrument has so soft and lovely a tone that nobody who has a heart can resist it."

Let's listen to the 2nd movement *adagio*, one of Mozart's all-time heavenly greats.

Take special note of how the double basses play starting at 01:55 and again at 06:00.

The first time through, they rise while the melody falls.
The second time, they fall with the melody.

And that second time falling manages to pierce the heart absolutely, demonstrating Mozart's simple yet profound taste.

Video 24: K. 622: *Clarinet Concerto in A* (II. Adagio, Shifrin)

Video 25: K. 622: *Clarinet Concerto in A* (complete, Stadler)

And here are the animated graph versions of the entire three-movement concerto, although by a different soloist and orchestra.

Video 26: K. 622: *Clarinet Concerto in A* (I. Allegro, animated graph)

Video 27: K. 622: *Clarinet Concerto in A* (II. Adagio, animated graph)

Video 28: K. 622: *Clarinet Concerto in A* (III. Presto, animated graph)

The clarinetist Marcel Maurice once said about this work,

> *"This is the music that they are going to play for me when I enter heaven, or wherever Mozart may be."*

Something about Mozart causes those who spend an extraordinary amount of time getting to know his music to make such profound announcements.

Robert Greenberg, in his Teaching Company course "The Concerto," states after playing the beginning of the 3rd movement of this concerto:

> "It took 4.6 billion years to create the genetic and environmental conditions necessary for Mozart to exist. It can be argued that his is the music of our universe, through which we can understand ourselves; it is eternal."

We now focus on hearing a special concerto for solo violin and viola with an orchestra, Mozart's *Sinfonia Concertante*.

In the process, we talk about *rhetoric*, and how Mozart presents a kind of conversation with his instruments.

Chapter 6

Hearing Mozart, Part 3:
Sinfonia Concertante

*"Mozart encompasses the entire domain of musical creation,
but I've got only the keyboard in my poor head."*
Frederic Chopin

Playlist 6: MarkAndreAlexander.com/One-Click-to-Mozart/
(8 videos, 1 hr 13 min)

**Mozart suffered both personal and professional disaster
during the year 1778, the year before he composed his great
Sinfonia Concertante.**

The 22-year-old spent the year mostly in Mannheim,
Germany, and Paris, France.

In Mannheim, he had fallen in love with a young Aloysia Weber, who rejected his marriage proposal. (Later, he would marry her sister Constanze.) In Paris, his mother suddenly died, he failed to get a position he sought, and he had no money.

Mozart returned to Salzburg in early 1779, to his father and to the archbishop, as concert master of the court orchestra. His two years back in Salzburg were not happy ones.

> *But despite his personal and professional pain,*
> *Mozart's music rose above the suffering.*

He wrote several symphonies and concertos, a mass, the great vocal composition *Vesperae solennes de confessore in C* (see Chapter 12), and the delightful *"Posthorn" Serenade.*

Listen to the 4th movement *rondo* of this serenade, with the playful flute, oboe, and horns:

Video 1: K. 320: *Serenade No. 9 in D* (Posthorn, IV. Rondo)

Or this 3rd movement *menuetto* from the *Divertimento in D* (a light chamber composition in several movements characterized for its lightness, its being "diverting"):

Video 2: K. 334: *Divertimento in D* (III. Menuetto)

Mozart's music continued to reside in its heavenly home.

Music scholars tell us that the time Mozart spent with German composers in Mannheim found its way into some of his Salzburg compositions of 1779.

We will look at one of these great German-influenced compositions, the *Sinfonia Concertante in E-flat* in three movements. We will examine it through the lens of *rhetoric*, the art of persuasion, often through public speaking.

Why?

Because classical rhetoric was seen as having parallels in classical music and its construction. Here's a thumbnail sketch of classical rhetoric.

Classical Rhetoric

> In the 4th century B.C., Aristotle formalized the study of rhetoric, "the art of persuasion," or more accurately as Aristotle defined it, "discovering in the particular case the available means of persuasion."
>
> In ancient Greece, public speaking was valued as a core skill for anyone engaged in public life: politicians, lawyers, lawmakers, poets, and playwrights. They all studied rhetoric to enhance their public speaking skills.
>
> By the Renaissance, rhetoric fully encompassed the written language as well as the spoken language.
>
> Rhetoric applies to three kinds of speeches or writing:
>
> 1. *Forensic rhetoric*—Judicial: Speech about the past (a lawyer uses this to argue what happened).
>
> 2. *Ceremonial rhetoric*—Executive: Speech about the present (a politician uses this to both praise and blame).
>
> 3. *Deliberative rhetoric*—Legislative: Speech about the future (a lawmaker uses this to argue or deliberate for or against a law).
>
> Poets, playwrights, and other artists use all three kinds.
>
> Rhetoric also involves three modes of persuasion: *Logical* (arguments using evidence and critical reasoning), *Emotional* (arguments stimulating passions, both

positive and negative), and *Ethical* (arguments building the credibility of the speaker or writer)

Rhetoric divides into three main parts when constructing a rhetorical work:

1. *Invention:* What is the content of the speech for a particular occasion?

2. *Arrangement:* How should the content be organized, and in what order should it be presented?

3. *Style:* What stylistic elements should be used? (choices of vocabulary, patterns and sounds of sentences, and figures of speech, such as analogy or metaphor)

By Shakespeare's time in the 16th century, rhetoric flowered, especially in matters of style. For example, Aristotle mentions fewer than two dozen figures of speech. Shakespeare uses over 150. Today we have defined nearly 200 figures of speech.

Figures of speech function as a kind of ornamentation. Here's the same thing stated without and then with figures of speech:

- (without) Life is challenging these days.

- (with) These are the times that try men's souls.

Rhetoric in Classical Music

How does classical rhetoric apply to classical music?

Like speeches, musical compositions in the classical style attempt to persuade the public to delight in the music, to be carried away by it in a variety of ways.

And just as importantly, for composers like Haydn, Mozart, and Beethoven, the audience was expected to marvel in how the musical "speech" was constructed.

Classical music raises to high art
musical invention, arrangement, and style.

Great composers apply musical figures of speech,
a kind of restrained musical ornamentation.

The Baroque style delighted in sometimes excessive ornamentation when compared to the Classical style. (Trills, complex variations on a theme, and so on.)

In some ways, the more extreme examples in Baroque style reflected the excesses of the Euphuistic style of John Lily during the England renaissance. (But let's not forget that Bach brought the Baroque style to high art, even within apparent excessive ornamentation. It was not excessive in Bach's day, about 1700-1750.)

Mozart's audience was often expected to be able to "hear" subtler musical ornamentation. And to understand the musical progression of a musical "speech."

Public speakers want the audience to appreciate the logic of their speeches, be moved emotionally, and see them as truly great speakers.

Musical modes of persuasion include the logical, emotional, and ethical.

Mozart would want an audience to appreciate the logical construction of his music, be moved by it emotionally, and then to be awed by his compositional and performance craft.

Mozart's father studied rhetoric as part of his musical studies. As in Shakespeare's time, classical education in Mozart's day required rhetoric as a natural part of education. There is a strong connection between the two.

> *The Mozartian consciousness is much like*
> *the Shakespearean consciousness.*
>
> *The more you understand one rhetorically,*
> *the more you can understand the other.*

And not surprisingly, Mozart loved Shakespeare for both his language and his drama.

In 1779, in Salzburg, the 23-year-old Mozart was ready to write a mature concerto that applied musical rhetoric in wonderful ways.

Sinfonia Concertante in E-flat, Introduction

Mozart's *Sinfonia Concertante in E-flat* is a concerto for orchestra and two solo instruments, violin and viola. Mozart seems to have liked the viola more than the violin. When he played in string quartets, he tended to play the viola.

Although this concerto is not intended to show off the two soloists, it does introduce an interesting new dynamic: not only soloist and orchestra, but also soloist and soloist, as well as two soloists and orchestra.

The *Sinfonia Concertante in E-flat* does have places where the soloists can display their virtuosity.

For this deep dive into music, we will focus on and break down the rhetorical "invention" and "arrangement" of the 1st movement *allegro maestoso*. We will more lightly touch the second two movements. (Note: The best performance on YouTube is broken down into two videos: The first, with the 1st and 2nd movements, and the second, with the 3rd movement.)

Sinfonia Concertante in E-flat, 1ˢᵗ movement

Watching this video aids the listener by tracking when key instruments are playing. You can hear more by seeing more.

The music starts at 01:05 with the orchestra playing the first of a series of beautiful and lyrical melodies. And reflections can be seen throughout:

Video 3 at 1:05: K. 364: *Sinfonia Concertante in E-flat* (I. Allegro Maestoso, Perlman/ Zuckerman)

For example, the violins play a melody at 01:55 that the double basses shortly reflect at 02:01.

At 02:15, the French horns and oboes have a conversation together, trading melodies back and forth.

Both soloists, violin and viola, come in together at 03:20, answering the orchestra. Then the real rhetorical conversation begins.

Once you begin to listen to Mozart as if his instruments were orators and conversationalists, more about the structure and the meaning of his music becomes clear. Seeing performers is another way, apart from reading a score, to recognize the structure of the music.

Imagine the conversation:

03:33 - the violin speaks, answered by the orchestra.

03:41 - the viola joins the conversation, with the violin harmonizing with the viola throughout, declaring the two aligned.

03:58 - the orchestra moves the conversation into a minor direction.

04:01 - the violin answers.

04:09 - the viola offers an extended answer.

04:25 - the orchestra responds with the same note seven times.

04:27 - the viola answers with the same note, but five times with the final two notes ascending, moving the conversation into a higher tone and back into the major key, setting up so that...

04:29 - ...the violin takes up the conversation. Notice the beauty of this move.

When played by inspired performers, this conversation becomes a living, breathing, and silky-smooth play among the soloists; they speak the same language, like a husband and wife who know each other so well, they can complete each other's sentences. Then...

04:42 - the violin sets up the viola, which takes back the conversation, emphasizing the musical point made by the violin.

05:05 - after the viola closes out the first part of the conversation, the violin strikes up the next part with even greater beauty.

05:13 - the viola reinforces the meaning, with an ornamental flourish at the end.

05:19 - the violin extends it and the viola responds in kind, extending it even further.

05:39 - the viola and violin speak in harmony.

06:08 - the orchestra takes up the conversation where the violin and viola left off.

06:39 - the violin offers a melancholy response.

07:02 - the orchestra responds in kind, persuaded.

07:14 - the viola continues with the melancholy conversation.

07:37 - the violin answers, speeds up, and rhetorically engages the viola in a back-and-forth that moves them out of melancholy and back into a highly reflective joy and beauty.

08:09 - the oboes and French horns offer their support as the violin and viola continue the conversation.

08:34 - and the orchestra is back where it began, the violin and viola easing in as they did before.

09:30 - the orchestra takes a second minor turn, and the viola answers followed by the violin, which takes it more quickly back into joy and beauty, insistent on where the conversation should go, and then...

09:57 - the orchestra again responds with the same note seven times, but this time...

09:59 - the violin, rather than the viola, answers with the same note five times with the final two notes ascending, passing back to the viola.

10:13 - the orchestra insists again with a note repeated seven times.

10:15 - the viola answers with the same note five times, then two ascending notes, sending it back to the violin, and together they keep the conversation positive and cheerful; the French horns echo their cheerfulness, going much farther than they had before.

12:04 - the orchestra picks up the cheer and sets up the soloists.

12:26 - the soloists start the cadenza and share their virtuosic moments in perfect union.

13:44 - the orchestra returns, in agreement, and both the orchestra and soloists end the conversation together at 14:22.

Sinfonia Concertante in E-flat, 2nd movement

Video 4 at 14:35: K. 364: *Sinfonia Concertante in E-flat* (II. Andante, Perlman/Zuckerman)

Mozart's 2nd movement is slower (as are all *andantes*), has darker tones, and displays a more theatrical feel. The violin and viola engage in some beautiful musical pairings, seeking a greater harmonious feeling (and requiring great skill from the performers to play as one).

Sinfonia Concertante in E-flat, 3rd movement

(NOTE: The 3rd movement actually begins near the end of Video 4. Video 5 starts about 30 seconds into the movement.)

Video 5: K. 364: *Sinfonia Concertante in E-flat* (III. Presto, Perlman/Zuckerman)

Mozart's final 3rd movement *presto* shifts into a charming playfulness, showing off the soloists with sometimes competitive, frenetic playing. The movement has the flair of a comic opera, perhaps presaging Mozart's eventual move to Vienna and comic operatic success.

MOZART AND GREAT MUSIC

In total, the *Sinfonia Concertante in E-flat* demonstrates that Mozart stood ready to handle the higher levels of composition, rhetoric, and taste that would be required for him to write the great chamber music, symphonies, and operas to come.

Next, we explore more issues with finding meaning in music, and how in the 20th century musical structures evolved from *tonal* to *atonal* where musical meanings appeared to be losing meaning altogether.

Extended Discussion

Listen to this piano piece and ask yourself, "Which of nature's creatures is this music portraying?" Close your eyes, and let the piano paint the picture:

Video 6: Edvard Grieg: *Lyric Pieces, Op. 43 No 1*

When I ask this question of an audience, usually only about one in ten pick it up immediately.

The piece is subtitled in German "Schmetterling," which means...butterfly.

Listen to the piece again. The meaning should now be much more obvious.

Composers consciously compose so that their instrumental voices convey meaning. One of the more interesting, if extreme, musical examples is American composer Charles Ives' *The Unanswered Question*.

Before reading on, please listen to this six-minute piece of music without judging it or resisting the apparent dissonance of some of the instruments. The reason for it makes perfect sense. Try to see if you can glean some kind of meaning from the apparent conversation going on:

Video 7: Charles Ives: *The Unanswered Question*

This music offers a 20th century existentialist example of the individual crying out to apparently non-responding universe. In his grand six-part Norton Lectures, *The Unanswered Question*, Leonard Bernstein brilliantly breaks down the conversation:

00:00 - the strings represent the universe, calm, beautiful, a background tapestry to the life in our world, playing throughout the piece, paying no attention to the conversation

01:29 - a single horn asks the question.

01:56 - the woodwinds attempt to answer.

02:14 - a single horn again asks the question.

02:31 - the woodwinds again try to answer.

02:57 - a single horn insists on asking the question.

03:12 - the woodwinds try again to answer.

03:37 - for the 4th time, the horn asks.

03:52 - the woodwinds answer, more strained.

04:15 - for the 5th time, the horn asks.

04:26 - the woodwinds try to answer, but at the end fade away as if they have given up.

4:48 - for the 6th time, the horn asks.

4:56 - the woodwinds answer frenetically, insistently, dogmatically, as if they cannot face the truth.

5:36 - for the final time, the horn asks the unanswered question; the woodwinds fail to respond, and the universe plays on as it fades into the background.

For Bernstein, Ives uses this music to ask the question, "Whither music?" That is, where is music going?

Up until the beginning of the 20th century, classical music was *tonal*, with dissonance introduced but with tonal structures always in place. With the 20th century came *atonal* music, music that contained notes that seem to have lost all tonal cohesion.

Many people today can listen to Mozart and Schubert and Wagner and Brahms and even Stravinsky, but shy away from Schoenberg or Weber, or much contemporary classical music.

Why?

Because it does not sound like music as much as badly tuned instruments trying to play together. It sounds like the woodwinds in *The Unanswered Question*.

And to be fair, to many in Mozart's audience, some of his music sounded dissonant and atonal, something their ears were not used to. Modern music. Pretentious music. Music that to our ears is perfectly tonal.

Such as the beginning of Mozart's famous "Dissonance" string quartet, the first 110 seconds:

Video 8: K. 465: *String Quartet No. 19 in C* (I. Adagio-Allegro)

Even by today's standards the opening could be considered modern, if not contemporary. To the ears in Mozart's time (except those of composers like Haydn and Beethoven), this music sounded like cats fighting.

*Mozart stayed within the conventions of the Classical Style
but stretched the ears of his audience in ways that
profoundly influenced composers who followed him.*

Let's now turn to some of Mozart's beautiful but sometimes more abstract and challenging music, his chamber music, particularly his string quartets and quintets.

Although this next chapter requires time and effort, the rewards promise to be staggering.

Chapter 7

Mozart's Chamber Music: "A Blessing of Inconceivable Richness"

"I tell you before God and as an honest man that your son is the greatest composer known to me in person or in name; he has taste and in addition the most profound and complete knowledge of composition." Franz Joseph Haydn, to Mozart's father, after listening to one of the six quartets Mozart dedicated to him

Playlist 7: MarkAndreAlexander.com/One-Click-to-Mozart/
(14 videos, 7 hrs 4 min)

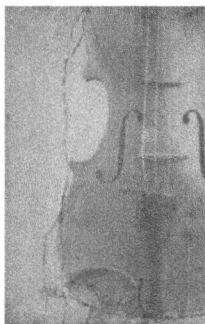

Chamber music is instrumental music written for one performer per line of music, unlike orchestras where many violins can play the same line of music, often in an intimate setting, like a salon or a parlor in an aristocratic home or palace.

Chamber music is music for the masses, who could not afford an orchestra but could get together in small groups and play.

Today, Mozart's chamber music, for two to five performers, is most often performed in small halls. (Other composers have composed works with many more performers.) Mozart's chamber output is phenomenal, over 100 works (25+ CDs), including:

Two string duos, nine piano duets, and thirty-eight sonatas and variations (violin, piano).

Three string trios, and five piano trios.

One oboe quartet, two piano quartets, four flute quartets, and twenty-three string quartets.

One clarinet quintet, two piano quintets, and six string quintets.

Chamber music requires different ears compared to orchestral music. When you listen to a piece of chamber music, you develop the ability to listen to each instrument individually. You recognize how that line of music weaves into the other lines of music.

Chamber music listening provides a multidimensional way of hearing music.

Yes, orchestral music does involve some multidimensional listening. But chamber music raises that listening to a new and distinct level.

The heavenly beauties in Mozart's chamber music reveal themselves to the devoted listener who builds the skill of listening multidimensionally; and it is a skill. With practice, you will discover the extraordinary value of this kind of listening.

Mozart became a permanent resident of Vienna at age 25, and during those years he wrote his finest chamber music. We will focus mainly on his mature works from this period.

Keep in mind that this chapter may best be worked through slowly and methodically over a period of weeks. There is a much depth here, and patience is required to retrieve its richness. In a larger book, this section may well have taken several chapters.

We start with an introduction via the kind of simpler chamber music that is easy to follow, yet mature and heavenly.

Violin Sonatas

Although a sonata indicates a solo instrument, in the case of violin sonatas the violin is accompanied by a piano. Listen to and watch the first of the three movements of Mozart's *Sonata for Violin and Piano in G* (ending at 8:32). Mozart composed this a few months before his mother died in 1778:

Video 1: K. 301: *Sonata for Violin and Piano in G*

Notice in chamber music how the performers play off of each other, sharing the melodies and harmonies. Mozart, even when he is composing two lines of music, displays his prowess in delightfully playing with the music.

Chamber musicians typically do not have a conductor, nor do they have a percussionist to keep the beat. So the performers must work together to keep the beat. Notice how Mozart provides that rhythm in the music itself.

Also, each time the main melody is repeated, notice how Mozart varies what the performers play.

00:04 - First, with violin

00:26 - Second, with piano

02:37 - Third, with violin (variation with piano)

03:00 - Fourth, with piano (variation with violin)

06:16 - Fifth, with piano and extremely varied violin that goes directly into...

06:31 - Sixth, with violin and more variation

Piano Trios

In the summer of 1788 in Vienna, Mozart experienced financial trouble. He needed money and, in the space of seven weeks from late June to early August, he wrote an incredible number of masterpieces. This was the kind of inhuman activity that had people labeling Mozart autistic, a god, or one who sold his soul to the devil.

They included: the Adagio and Fugue in C minor for string quartet (K. 546), a violin sonata (K. 547), two songs (K. 549, K. 552), two piano sonatas (K. 545, K. 547a), and on top of all that his three great symphonies, No. 39, No. 40 in G minor, and No. 41, the "Jupiter" (K. 543, K. 550, K. 551).

He also composed two piano trios (K. 542, K. 548) for piano, violin, and cello.

We will listen to Mozart's Piano Trio in E. This piece would be classed by some as "serious" music, since it does not have the immediacy of a hummable, delightful melody. However, it serves as a visual and auditory example of how Mozart composes three lines of melody that fully takes advantage of the three instruments.

Listen to and watch the 7-minute 1st movement that starts at 01:00. (If you prefer something lighter, try the 2nd movement that begins at 7:59, or for something more fun and melodic, try the 3rd movement that begins at 13:18.)

This video is particularly well directed in how it shows the interplay of the three instruments, the piano, the violin, and the cello:

Video 2: K. 542: *Piano Trio in E*

String Quartets

Quartets add further complexity to the interplay of instruments. String quartets have four lines of music: a first violin, a second violin, a viola, and a cello. They also have four movements.

Mozart met Joseph Haydn in 1781, when the older man was 49 years old. Despite the 24-year difference in age, the two became mutual admirers and friends. Mozart said that he learned how to compose string quartets from Haydn alone.

Haydn presented his String Quartets Op. 33 (nicknamed the Russian quartets) as written in a new and specific manner. The musical lines displayed a level of independence that turned them into characters who seem to be having a musical conversation. Haydn also constantly transformed and organically grew the musical ideas in these quartets.

Mozart took Haydn's pioneering efforts and elevated them to sheer genius.

Over a two-year period ending in January 1885, Mozart wrote six famous string quartets dedicated to Haydn (K. 387, K. 421, K. 428, K. 458, K. 464, K. 465). He was the one composer whom Mozart most respected, and Mozart knew "Papa Haydn" would grasp the delicacies of his particular compositions.

Here is Mozart's published dedication page:

To my dear friend Haydn,

A father who had resolved to send his children out into the great world took it to be his duty to confide them to the protection and guidance of a very celebrated Man, especially when the latter by good fortune was at the same time his best Friend. Here they are then, O great Man and dearest Friend, these six children of mine. They are, it is true, the fruit of a long and laborious endeavor, yet the hope inspired in me by several Friends that it may be at least partly compensated encourages me, and I flatter myself that this offspring will serve to afford me solace one day. You, yourself, dearest friend, told me of your satisfaction with them during your last Visit to this Capital. It is this indulgence above all which urges me to commend them to you and encourages me to hope that they will not seem to you altogether unworthy of your favour. May it therefore please you to receive them kindly and to be their Father, Guide and Friend! From this moment I resign to you all my rights in them, begging you however to look indulgently upon the defects which the partiality of a Father's eye may have concealed from me, and in spite of them to continue in your generous Friendship for him who so greatly values it, in expectation of which I am, with all of my Heart, my dearest Friend, your most Sincere Friend,

W. A. Mozart

The first of these six, the *String Quartet #14 in G* composed in December 1782, is light and fresh, and foreshadows some of Mozart's mature music to follow. The four-note theme in the 4th movement of Mozart's Jupiter symphony, for example, appears first here in the quartet's 4th movement.

Robert Greenberg declares it "miracle of technique, taste, and imagination":

Video 3: K. 387: *String Quartet No. 14 in G*

00.00: I. *Allegro vivace assai*
08.05: II. *Menuetto, allegro - trio*
16.50: III. *Andante cantabile*
24.35: IV. *Molto allegro*

Mozart composed the *String Quartet No. 15 in D minor* six months later in June 1783, when his wife went into labor. She claimed that Mozart composed her labor pains into the opening movement.

Mozart continued to push the edge of music with this quartet. His fellow composers criticized him for being too artful, difficult, and problematic, partly because this and the other Haydn quartets all contain a high level of chromaticism (using all the notes in an octave, especially rising and falling combinations of neighboring notes, often five or more in a row).

The 3rd movement displays a particularly playful *pizzicato* (where the performers pluck their instruments.)

The final dance-like movement shows how Mozart can vary the same theme in endless ways, a style Beethoven noted and extended even further:

Video 4: K. 421: *String Quartet No. 15 in D minor*

00.00: I. *Allegro moderato*
08.22: II. *Andante*
15.38: III. *Menuetto, Allegretto - Trio*
19.48: IV. - *Allegretto ma non troppo - Più allegro*

Mozart's third string quartet dedicated to Haydn, the *String Quartet No. 16 in E-flat* also composed in the summer of 1783, is probably the most emotionally strained while still being lyrical and full of surprises.

All four movements display Mozart stretching his harmonic forms, struggling to find new depths of musical expression:

Video 5: K. 428: *String Quartet No. 16 in E-flat*

00.00: I. *Allegro non troppo*
08.05: II. *Andante con moto*
15.28: III. *Menuetto, Allegro - Trio*
21.28: IV. *Allegro vivace*

The *String Quartet No. 17 in B-flat*, nicknamed The Hunt, is one of Mozart's most splendid chamber compositions. The nickname comes from the opening of the first theme, which provides an almost horn-like announcement for a hunt.

Haydn made his famous remarks, at the beginning of this chapter, after listening to this and the final two of the six quartets. Boisterous, high-spirited, engaging without being too emotional, this work is a joy from beginning to end:

Video 6: K. 458: *String Quartet No. 17 in B-flat*

00.00: I. *Allegro vivace assai*
08.51: II. *Menuetto, Moderato - Trio*
13.19: III. *Adagio*
20.44: IV. *Allegro assai*

Mozart's *String Quartet No. 18 in A* moved Beethoven to say to Carl Czerny,

> *"What a work.*
> *It was here that Mozart said to the world,*
> *Behold what I might have done for you*
> *if the time were right."*

Beethoven copied out by hand the 4th movement *allegro non troppo*, one that profoundly influenced his own musical style for decades to come.

This is perhaps the most intense and complex of the Haydn quartets, full of contrapuntal passages (passages where two lines of music provide different contrasting melodies):

Video 7: K. 464: *String Quartet No. 18 in A*

00.00: I. *Allegro*
07.38: II. *Menuetto - Trio*
13.58: III. *Andante*
25.30: IV. *Allegro non troppo*

The String Quartet No. 19 in C, nicknamed The Dissonance, starts off with an unusually dissonant, dark, almost modern prologue, before breaking into the kind of light upbeat melody we come to expect from Mozart.

Composers and the public at the time thought Mozart violated the rules of appropriate musical expression and taste with this quartet. Not long after these quartets were published, Mozart descended into financial and emotional desperation. He had less than six years to live.

Today, the Dissonance quartet is viewed as one of Mozart's most fluid works, which effortlessly combines both bright and shadowy textures. One can only imagine Haydn's amazement and delight after the conclusion:

Video 8: K. 465: *String Quartet No. 19 in C* **(The Dissonance)**

00.00: I. *Adagio - Allegro*
11.56: II. *Andante cantabile*
19.35: III. *Menuetto, Allegro - Trio*
24.58: IV. *Allegro molto*

Piano Quartets and Quintets

Written in 1785, Mozart's *Piano Quartet in G minor* caused British musicologist Hans Keller to write:

> *"The piano quartet K. 478 in G minor*
> *furnishes conclusive proof, more than*
> *any other single masterpiece of his,*
> *that Mozart's was the only truly*
> *omniscient ear of which we know."*

What an extraordinary statement!

This work blends the public and private Mozart, making virtuosic demands of the pianist in the same way as did his public piano concertos:

Video 9: K. 478: *Piano Quartet in G minor*

00.00: I. *Allegro*
14.15: II. *Andante*
21.10: III. *Rondo (Allegro)*

Mozart wrote the following *Piano and Wind Quintet in E-flat* in 1784. He thought so much of it that he wrote his father saying,

> *"I consider it to be the best work*
> *I have ever composed."*

The young Beethoven admired this work so much that he created one for the same set of instruments in the exact same key. (This explains why you will find recordings of both on many of the same CDs.)

Video 10: K. 452 *Piano and Wind Quintet in E-flat*

00.00: I. *Largo - Allegro moderato*
10:00: II. *Larghetto*
18:30: III. *Allegretto*

String Quintets

Mozart wrote six four-movement string quintets, the first in Salzburg when he was 17 years old. The first of these quintets shows youthful exuberance, even in its softer moments. Pay particular attention to the fresh and brilliant 3rd movement:

> **Video 11: K. 174: *String Quintet No. 1 in B-flat* (complete)**
>
> 00.00: I. *Allegro moderato*
> 08.47: II. *Adagio*
> 14.21: III. *Menuetto ma allegretto*
> 18.14: IV. *Allegro*

But Mozart is most famous for his two string quintets written in Vienna in the spring of 1787 when he was 31 years old, Nos. 3 and 4. The addition of a viola to the standard string quartet provided Mozart with added expressive power, one step closer to a string orchestra. Yet the music is still intimate.

Though Mozart expect his string quintets to sell well, they did not. Such uncompromising masterpieces seemed beyond the ears of the time.

The *String Quintet No. 3 in C* is Mozart's longest four-movement work.

The 1st movement *allegro* presents the cello engaging in conversation with the first violin, in a kind of call-and-response style.

The 2nd movement *menuetto - allegretto* stands out for its multiple combinations of instruments. Listen for how Mozart combines them in all kinds of ways.

The 3rd movement *Andante* is serious and expressive, and the 4th movement *allegro* is lively, light, and full of musical maturity:

Video 12: K. 515: *String Quintet No. 3 in C*

00.00: I. *Allegro*
13.19: II. *Menuetto - Allegretto*
18.55: III. *Andante*
27.15: IV. *Allegro*

The *String Quintet No. 4 in G minor* is regarded by some as the most powerful piece of music that Mozart composed. Its challenges for the new listener are extraordinary. In some ways, it is the Everest of chamber pieces.

Darker, richer, at times rough and sad, and other times lighter and even frisky. There is little one can say about this music. There is nothing like it, except to say that it is exceptionally Mozart:

Video 13: K. 516: *String Quintet No. 4 in G minor*

00.00: I. *Allegro*
08.06: II. *Menuetto - Allegretto*
13.17: III. *Adagio ma non troppo*
21.48: IV. *Adagio - Allegro*

Just months before his death, Mozart wrote the last movement of his final string quintet, which was his final work of chamber music. He wrote as if he had a long life to come:

Video 14: K. 614: *String Quintet No. 6 in E-flat* (IV. Allegro)

Chapter 8

Hearing Mozart, Part 4: Singular, Idiosyncratic, and Special-Occasion Gems

"A light, bright, fine day this will remain throughout my whole life. As from afar, the magic notes of Mozart's music still gently haunt me. A world that has produced a Mozart is a world worth saving. What a picture of a better world you have given us, Mozart!"
Franz Schubert

Playlist 8: MarkAndreAlexander.com/One-Click-to-Mozart/
(20 videos, 4 hrs 48 min)

Mozart loved play and exercising his musical curiosity, so not surprisingly he crafted some unusual and idiosyncratic pieces of music.

Leopold Mozart died in Salzburg on May 28, 1787. He left nothing to his son. Mozart's sister, Marianne, had inherited it all, including some of Mozart's scores left in his father's hands. In other words, all of the money that Mozart had earned in his childhood and youth that Leopold had taken was denied him.

We have no record of how Mozart felt about his father's death. We do, however, have a record of how he felt about his pet bird, a starling that died three days after his father. Mozart wrote a eulogy for it:

A silly fool lies here
One whom I held so dear—
A starling in his prime
During such a brief time
Whose fate it was to drain
Death's harsh and acrid pain.
Thinking on this, my heart
Is ripped and wrenched apart.
Dear reader, shed a tear,
As you overlook here.
He was not wicked, quite,
But happy, glad and bright,
And underneath his brag
He was a silly wag.
This no one can deny
And point out now, say I
That he resides on high,
And from that lovely sky,
Praises me without pay
In his kind and sweet way.
But heedless of his death
He's breathed his final breath,
And thinks not of this one
Whose rhyme is forthwith done.

Perhaps Mozart's eulogy to his father came, not in words, but in the first work he composed shortly after hearing of his father's death.

A Musical Joke

Mozart's superior compositional experience and taste meant that, in the musical world of Vienna circa 1787, he would have been confronted with a range of fawning pretenders to compositional talent.

Although his father had talent as a composer, Mozart would not have been above making fun of the kinds of forms his father taught him, and which Mozart had long since surpassed.

Ein Musikalischer Spaß (A Musical Joke) makes fun of those composers and performers who lack taste and talent.

This four-movement work is laugh-out-loud funny to classical musicians.

Here are some of the jokes to listen for: banal melodies, amateurish repetition of simplistic phrases, clumsy variations on a theme, bizarre harmonic progressions, and passages of bad virtuosic scales.

Also listen for musicians who simply cannot play well. For example, in the 2nd movement at 5:08 and 9:55, Mozart makes fun of amateur horn players. And at the very end of the final movement, the performers break down completely after an unnecessary series of bad race-car-like *presto* passages.

Listen, laugh, and enjoy:

Video 1: K. 522: *Ein Musikalischer Spaß (A Musical Joke*, complete)

00.00: I. *Allegro*
04.22: II. *Menuetto (Maestoso) - Trio*
11.18: III. *Adagio Cantabile*
16.24: IV. *Presto*

A Musical Dice Game

In our day, software programmers have played with the idea of computers generating random music according to certain rules. Mozart also played with the idea of using dice to randomly generate waltzes from a set of two-bar musical fragments.

Mozart was not the first. The 18th century provides plenty examples of games throughout Western Europe that randomly generated music.

Mozart must have been in a playful mood after his father's death, since this musical dice game was also composed in 1787. Here we have Erik Smith, a harpsichordist, and conductor Sir Neville Marriner together talking us through the rolls of the dice to generate the sequence of fragments from Mozart's score.

Erik Smith plays the randomly generated composition near the end at 6:20:

Video 2: K. 516f: *A Musical Dice Game*

Works for Glass Harmonica

Mozart composed for whatever instruments and performers were available. As new instruments were invented or improved, Mozart took notice.

The glass harmonica is something almost everyone is familiar with in its original form. An Irish musician in the 1740s performed on glass goblets filled with varying amounts of water. He generated tones by rubbing his fingers around the ends.

Benjamin Franklin worked with a glassblower in London to create a new design of thirty-seven bowls arranged horizontally on an iron spindle. (You can see "Franklin's Armonica" on Wikipedia.)

The glass harmonica is an entertaining instrument in small doses, but like all confections proves to be somewhat nauseating when indulged. Not surprisingly, it never became a popular instrument.

In 1791, the year of his death, Mozart composed two short works for glass harmonica, probably in an attempt to take advantage of its temporary popularity.

Mozart wrote this four-minute adagio with two lines of music for glass harmonica only:

Video 3: K. 356: *Adagio in C* (for glass harmonica)

Mozart wrote this 12-minute adagio and rondo as a quintet in two movements for flute oboe, clarinet, violin, cello, and glass harmonica:

Video 4: K. 617: *Adagio and Rondo* (for glass harmonica)

00.00: I. *Adagio*
04.15: II. *Rondo: Allegretto*

Music for Pantomime

Mozart's sister-in-law who sang soprano in Vienna, Aloysia Weber, was married to Joseph Lange, who became a friend of Mozart's. Both he and Mozart were Masons, members of a fraternal order founded in the 15th century and still existing today.

Lange played a part in a "masquerade" by Mozart composed in 1783 for Carnival, a masked celebration common to many cultures. In Vienna this would most be likely performed in an aristocratic household, possibly with members of the household participating.

The characters were traditional figures of the *commedia dell'arte*, a staple of Italian acting festivals. The characters wore masks and did not speak.

In this piece, Lange played the character Pierrot and Mozart played the standard character of "Harlequin."

This beautiful eight-movement work for chamber orchestra makes us wish we could see the masquerade that went with it. It provides both light and dark passages, but all with a festive air:

Video 5: K. 446: *Music to a Pantomime*

00.00: I. *Overture: Allegro*
03.30: II. *Allegro - Maestoso - Allegro*
07.30: III. *Poco adagio - Andante molto*
09.31: IV. *Adagio - Allegro - Allegro assai*
14.24: V. *Allegro maestoso - Larghetto*
17.39: VI. *Allegro - Maestoso*
21.56: VII. *Allegro - Marcia: Maestoso quasi marcia funebre*
26.33: VIII. *Finale: Presto*

Piano Pieces

When people think of Beethoven, they often think of a man alone at the piano. Beethoven was well-known for his solo piano pieces, such as *Für Elise, Moonlight Sonata,* and the like.

When people think of Mozart, they rarely think of him as a composer of solo piano pieces. Students of the piano invariably get to play some, but when it comes to solo keyboard music,

Bach, Beethoven, and Schubert are the standouts in the 18th and early-19th centuries.

Where Beethoven wrote over one hundred piano sonatas, some of the most interesting and demanding pieces for concert pianists, Mozart wrote eighteen.

Mozart's *Piano Sonata No. 16 in E-flat* is the best introduction to his piano sonatas. Apparently, he wrote it for his students to exercise their fingers, but even as an exercise, Mozart could not help but write heavenly music. Pay particular attention to the sublime 2nd movement *andante*:

Video 6: K. 545: *Piano Sonata No. 16 in E-flat* (Warren)

00.00: I. *Allegro*
04.40: II. *Andante*
11.40: III. *Rondo*

In 1786, Mozart composed an astonishing piano duet where two performers sat at the same piano. Of the *Sonata for Piano in F Four Hands*, British musicologist Donald Tovey said that "four Chinese dragons might achieve its august poise and agility":

Video 7: K. 497: *Sonata for Piano in F Four-Hands*

00.27: I. *Adagio - Allegro di molto*
13.35: II. *Andante*
28:47: III. *(Allegro)*

Masonic Music

Mozart became a member of the Masonic Order at 28 years old, seven years before his death. After that time, many of his friends were Masons. Not surprisingly, freemasonry influenced much of his music in the latter part of his life.

Freemasonry espoused Enlightenment-inspired humanist views, particularly the idea that nobility of the spirit was not limited by social rank. Masons believed that people of lower classes could be noble in spirit just as those of higher ranks could be mean in spirit, a theme of some of Mozart's operas.

Masons used music in their ceremonies, and Mozart naturally provided some of their finest music. Here is a short, beautiful work of funeral music:

Video 8: K. 477: *Maurerische Trauermusik* (Masonic Funeral Music)

Mozart composed another short work, the "*Little Masonic Cantata*," in Vienna one month before his death, for the opening of the temple of the New Crowned Hope Masonic Lodge. This appears to be Mozart's last complete work; his *Requiem in D minor* was left incomplete at his death:

Video 9: K. 623: *Eine Kleine Freimaurer Cantate (Little Masonic Cantata)*

00.00: I. *Allegro*
01.27: II. *Accompagnato*
03.52: III. *Andante*
07.07: IV. *Accompagnato*
08.15: V. *Andante*
10.56: VI. *Allegro*

Here is a list of some of Mozart's other masonic music:

K. 53 *Lied: An die Freude* A masonic poem
K. 93 Psalm 129: *De Profundis Clamavi*
K. 148 *O Heiliges Band* (Hallowed bond of friendship)
K. 273 *Graduale ad Festum B.M.V.: "Sancta Maria, mater Die*
K. 345 *Thamos Konig in Agypten* (Thamos, King of Egypt)

K. 410 *Canonic Adagio* for 2 bassett horns and bassoon.
K. 411 *Adagio for 2 Clarinets and 3 Bassett Horns*
K. 429 *Cantata: Dir, Seele des Weltalls*
K. 468 *Gesellenreise.* (Fellow Craft's Journey)
K. 471 Cantata: *Die Maurerfreude* (Masonic Joy)
K. 483 *Zerfließet heut, geliebte Brüder*
K. 484 *Ihr unsre neuen Leiter*
K. 543 *Symphony No. 39 in E-flat.* (Alfred Einstein writes of this symphony's masonic significance in his book *Mozart: His Character, His Work)*
K. 617 *Adagio and Rondo for Flute, Oboe, Viola, Cello, and Celesta*
K. 619 *Cantata: Die ihr des unermeßlichen Weltalls Schöpfer ehrt*
K. 620 *Die Zauberflöte (The Magic Flute)*
K. 623b Chorus: "Lasst uns mit geschlungen Handen"

Dance Music

Mozart loved to dance. He wrote a great amount of dance music in the form of minuets, German dances, and contredanses. Generally, Mozart wrote dance music for specific occasions.

Dance music is naturally shorter, lighter fare in keeping with the need for the dancers at balls to be at ease as they dance.

Here is Mozart's final minuet:

Video 10: K. 604: *Minuet No. 2 in E-flat*

Here is Mozart's final contredanse:

Video 11: K. 610: *Contredanse for orchestra in G* ("La filles malicieuses")

And here is Mozart's final German dance:

Video 12: K. 611: *German Dance for orchestra in C*

Arias for Special Occasions

Sometimes between the acts of an opera, a special solo *aria* was presented unrelated to the opera. At other times vocalists, both male and female, would commission a composer to write an aria or song that showed off their vocal abilities. Occasionally, a publisher would commission a work for publication.

Mozart wrote many arias and songs for such occasions. Here's one he wrote in German for his sister-in-law, Aloysia Weber, whom he once expected to marry, with English translation:

> Thanks dear friends, I sing it loudly,
> as fervent as my heart can cry.
> We man may sing such praises proudly,
> but woman's voice must gently fly.
>
> Know my memory will stay forever,
> loved for kindness shown a friend;
> I would wait for you wherever,
> serving you to the joyous end!
>
> Since creation, the Fates decreed
> that artists consistently must roam,
> and so with me, by Muses indeed,
> I leave my native land and home.
>
> My destiny has thus ordained it.
> In every land that calls, it's smart
> that where I go, I shall confess it,
> Your hands will ever hold my heart.

Video 13: K. 383: *"Nehmt meinen Dank"*

Mozart wrote this Italian aria, also sung by Aloysia Weber, for insertion in an opera by Pasquale Anfossi, *Il curioso indiscreto*, which premiered in 1777 in Rome. The text derives from Cervantes' *Don Quixote.*

> Let me say, dear Lord,
> The nature of my grief!
> But destiny condemns me
> To cry, yet stay silent.
>
> My heart may not yearn
> For the lover I would love
> Making me seem stubborn,
> harsh, and cruel.
>
> Ah, Count, leave me,
> Run, take flight
> Away from me;
> The one you love,
> Emilia, looks for you,
> Let her not ache,
> She deserves your love.
>
> Ah, shameless stars!
> You favor me not.
> I am lost when he remains.
>
> Flee from me, run,
> Speak not of this love,
> Her heart belongs to you.

Video 14: K. 418: *"Vorrei spiegarvi"*

Here is the translation of the Italian lyrics for the final *aria* written Mozart ever wrote for a Bass vocalist:

> By this honest hand,
> by these endearing eyes,
> I am foresworn, darling,
> that none shall I love but you.

The air, the earth, the rocks themselves,
knowing my sighs, hearing them well,
will speak to you
how I am constant and true.

Turn your sunny eyes on me
and say whether you despise or love me.

Ever ignited by your tender looks,
Please call me yours forever.

Neither the heavens nor the earth can change
that love dwelling within my heart.

Video 15: K. 612: *Aria for Bass, "Per questa bella mano"*

And here's one commissioned by a publisher for a book of children's songs, with a translation of the German lyrics:

We children touch many pleasures,
We joke and flirt only in play;
We are noisy with our singing and running around,
Hopping and jumping in the grass.

Hey brothers, jump and curl in the grass!
It's still permitted do so, and it's appropriate for us!
For when we get older, the times do change,
When we walk more stiff and slowly.

But wait, the sun has set so early?
But we are still playing, dear sun, forgive us!
Until tomorrow, dear brothers, sleep well and good
night!
Yes, tomorrow we again will laugh and dance and play.

Video 16: K. 598: *Song, "Das Kinderspiel"* (Children's Games)

Organ Music

Although Mozart wrote many shorter church sonatas and other pieces for organ, he wrote one that is magnificent, even for those who have never liked organ music.

The *Fantasia in F minor for mechanical organ* shows that Bach continued to influence Mozart even in his final year on this earth. Count Joseph Deym von Strzitez commissioned this work for a mausoleum that opened in Vienna in 1791 for Field-Marshal Baron con Loudon.

Mozart called the mechanical organs in his day "little pipes that sound too childish for me." Mozart found writing such funeral music bothersome, but he needed the money.

He managed to push through his boredom with the piece, and he still achieved creating a masterpiece.

Here is a version played on the great organ at Notre Dame in France. This would have been more like what Mozart sought for an organ piece.

Video 17: K. 608: *Fantasia in F minor for mechanical organ*

The Great Mass in C minor

Mozart composed fifteen complete settings of the Mass Ordinary for chorus, soloists, and orchestra between the years 1768-1780.

In 1782, when he was no longer a church musician in Salzburg, he swore that he would write a new mass for his soon-to-be wife, Constance. No one knows why it was unfinished.

Despite its incomplete status, the *Great Mass in C minor* is a profoundly moving work, scored for two soprano soloists, a tenor, and a bass.

The large-scale work is broken down into the following movements:

Kyrie: chorus and soprano

Gloria:
- Gloria in excelsis Deo: chorus
- Laudamus te: soprano
- Gratias agimus tibi; chorus
- Domine Deus: sopranos
- Qui tollis: double choir
- Quoniam tu solus: sopranos
- Jesu Christe: chorus
- Cum Sancto Spiritu: chorus

Credo (incomplete):
- Credo in unum Deum: chorus
- Et incarnatus est: soprano

Sanctus (incomplete):
- Sanctus: double choir
- Benedictus qui venit: quartet and double chorus

In July of 2015, Pope Francis stated,

*"Among musicians I love Mozart, of course.
The 'Et incarnatus est' from his Mass in C minor is matchless;
it lifts you to God!"*

Video 18: K. 427: *Great Mass in C minor*

Requiem

Finally, we come to Mozart's *Requiem in D minor*, a work mostly unfinished at the time of his death. The commission and composing of the *Requiem in D minor* were strange for a couple of reasons:

> 1. Mozart was commissioned to compose this work by someone unknown to him, and no completion date was required. But Mozart thought it would take him four weeks. He was paid one hundred ducats for the commission and began composing immediately.

> 2. He was in poor health, fainting often while working. He with his wife, Constanze, felt that this work was for his own funeral, admitting he was having "very strange thoughts."

The work was actually commissioned through intermediaries by an eccentric count, Franz von Walsegg, well known for commissioning works and passing them off as his own.

Mozart completed only the opening movement, the *Requiem aeternam*. The other movements were either not started or barely outlined, while others were only partially complete. Constanze gave the manuscript to the composer Franz Xaver Süssmayr, to complete. This is the version most people hear today.

Since it is the only part of the *Requiem in D minor* Mozart completed, let's listen to the first movement. The video includes the lyrics sung by the choir:

Video 19: K. 626: *Requiem in D minor* (I. Requiem aeternam)

If you would like to hear the full *Requiem in D minor*, which includes Süssmayr's completions, here is a fine live recording. I've included links to each movement:

Video 20: K. 626: *Requiem in D minor*

01:00: Introitus
05:56: Kyrie
08:19: Dies irae
10:17: Tuba mirum
14:05: Rex tremendae
16:01: Recordare
21:20: Confutatis
23:56: Lacrimosa
27:48: Domine Jesu Christe
31:10: Hostias
34:50: Sanctus
36:36: Benedictus
42:12: Agnus Dei
46:21: Lux aeterna

Mozart died December 5, 1791. He worked on the *Requiem* between October 8 and November 20, but was then confined to his bed and died two weeks later just after midnight.

That night, Mozart said to his sister-in-law Sophie, "Ah, dearest Sophie how glad I am that you have come. You must stay tonight and watch me die."

Next, we move from the small chamber works to Mozart's larger symphonies. Though not as large as Beethoven's, Mozart's symphonies paved the way for all those that followed.

Chapter 9

Mozart's Symphonies

"His imagination is as musical as his ear; it always hears many sounds together; one sound heard recalls instantaneously all those that may form a melodious sequence and a complete symphony."
August Tissot, 1766

Playlist 9: MarkAndreAlexander.com/One-Click-to-Mozart/
(13 videos, 6 hrs 37 min)

During the summer of 1788, three years before his death, Mozart composed his three great symphonies over a period of six weeks, and no one knows why.

Mozart almost always composed for a purpose, for a commission, at someone's behest. But these three symphonies, Mozart's last, appeared mysteriously without apparent reason or record of why he composed them.

First, some basics. The word "symphony" (from the Italian *sinfonia*, referring to an opera overture) does *not* refer to a large group of instruments being played together. That collection is called an "orchestra."

A symphony is a musical form with multiple movements founded during the Classical era by Haydn and Mozart. It began with three movements with Haydn and Mozart's early symphonies, but evolved into four movements with different moods, broken down into the following four styles:

1st movement: Intellectual and challenging (often the longest of the four movements)

2nd movement: Lyrical and moderate

3rd movement: Dance-like and upbeat

4th movement: Playful and fast

Entertaining orchestral music became most popular with middle-class audiences in the late 18th century, a time when Haydn and Mozart perfected the symphony.

Later composers, like Beethoven and Schubert, stayed within Classical-era structures with their early symphonies, while their later symphonies brought more expressive power. Composers of the Romantic era, especially Brahms, Berlioz, and finally Mahler, expanded the number and length of movements.

For Haydn and Mozart, symphonies typically ranged from twenty to thirty minutes. Later composers began expanding that to forty-five or even sixty minutes and longer.

To many, Mahler essentially ended the symphony by making it "the world," composing vast 90-minute symphonies and increasing the size of the orchestra. His *Symphony No. 8* was nicknamed the "Symphony of a Thousand" for the grand number of instruments and vocalists (conceiving it as a "new symphonic universe," a synthesis of symphony, cantata (a choir work with accompanying instruments), oratorio (a large-scale work for orchestra, choir, and soloists), motet (a highly varied choral music), and lied (a song of a German poem set to music).)

But in the late 18th century, the symphony was more modest.

Mozart's Early Symphonies

Mozart wrote the first 24 of his 41 numbered symphonies before he turned 18 years old. (He wrote another dozen during that time, which were not numbered. And of the 41, No. 3 was written by his father, and No. 37, by Michael Haydn, to which Mozart added a slow introduction.)

It was with the 20-minute *Symphony No. 25 in G minor* that we first glimpse the great Mozartian symphonies to come. This is an astonishing composition given Mozart's young age at 16. You may remember the opening 1st movement music from the film *Amadeus*:

> **Video 1: K. 183: *Symphony No. 25 in G minor* (complete)**
>
> 00.00: *Allegro con brio*
> 07.40: *Andante*
> 11.42: *Menuetto & Trio*
> 15.15: *Allegro*

Symphony No. 25 is nicknamed the "little G minor" symphony, given that the other G minor symphony, No. 40, overshadows all of Mozart's symphonies.

Another example of an early symphony, written in Salzburg when Mozart was 18, is the *Symphony No. 29 in A*. The Mozart biographer Maynard Solomon holds up the 1st movement of this symphony as one of the "few exceptions" when he says:

Mozart's mature instrumental music represents our
civilization's sign for the beautiful. We cannot think of
him without thinking of beauty; We cannot refer to
beauty without recalling his music. I believe this is so,
not necessarily because his works are more beautiful
than those of other composers, though this may well be
true, but because he created—or, at least, brought into
the forefront of aesthetic consciousness—a special kind
of musical beauty, one that thenceforth came to
exemplify the idea of superlative beauty itself. There are
many beauties in Mozart's earlier works as well, but with
few exceptions...they are missing the excruciating,
surplus quality that transforms loveliness into ecstasy,
grace into sublimity, pleasure into rapture. (Chapter 24
in *Mozart: A Life*)

What a fine distinction between what makes Mozart's works
great vs. timeless:

> *"...the excruciating, surplus quality*
> *that transforms loveliness into ecstasy,*
> *grace into sublimity,*
> *pleasure into rapture."*

This recording is unusual in how it gives you four views of
the orchestra performing this symphony. The 1st movement
allegro moderato represents the quality Solomon speaks of:

Video 2: K. 201: *Symphony No. 29 in A* (complete)

00.00: *Allegro moderato*
07.10: *Andante*
12.20: *Menuetto: Allegretto - Trio*
15.20: *Allegro con spirito*

Mozart's Later Symphonies

Before writing his final three great symphonies, with the final two being truly timeless, Mozart wrote about a half dozen symphonies that demonstrated increasing maturity.

Mozart wrote *Symphony No. 35 in D*, the "Haffner" symphony, when he was 26 and living in Vienna. It's named after the Haffner family of Salzburg. (Six years earlier Mozart wrote another work named after the same family, the beautiful "Haffner Serenade" K. 250.)

Video 3: K. 385: *Symphony No. 35 in D* (Haffner, complete)

00.00: *Allegro con spirito*
05:30: *Andante*
14.14: *Menuetto*
17:40: *Presto*

One year later, Mozart wrote his next symphony, *Symphony No. 36 in C*, nicknamed the "Linz" since that is the city where he wrote it. He wrote it in four days:

Video 4: K. 425: *Symphony No. 36 in C* (Linz, complete)

00.00: *Adagio - Allegro spiritoso*
10:50: *Andante con moto*
18.18: *Menuetto*
22.12: *Presto*

A year later in Vienna, while Mozart prepared to travel to Prague, he wrote the *Symphony No. 38 in D*, which he would conduct in Prague one month later. He was also working on one of the great operas of all time, *Don Giovanni*, which would debut ten months later. The depth of emotion Mozart displayed while writing that opera shows up in this symphony as well.

The symphony has three movements only (there is no minuet or trio), and the depth of emotion is apparent from the beginning. The first few minutes of the 1st movement function as a kind of overture to the entire movement as Mozart moves between major and minor keys. Anyone familiar with *Don Giovanni* can sense it lurking in the musical background.

The 1st movement takes nearly half of the entire 29-minute symphony, and generates increasing intensity through the use of counterpoint (very different, independent, and harmonious musical lines) and polyphony (two or more simultaneous lines of independent melody).

The 2nd movement, though a slower *andante*, maintains the intensity and achieves a stellar degree of expressive perfection.

The 3rd movement, rousing and fast like many Mozart finales, provides many themes and combinations of instruments:

Video 5: K. 504: *Symphony No. 38 in D* (Prague, complete)

00.00: *Adagio - Allegro*
14.00: *Andante*
22.55: *Finale Presto*

Mozart would not write another symphony until eighteen months later, and we are the poorer for it. For in the *Symphony No. 38 in D*, written in 1786, we hear the growing expressive maturity that will launch into a timeless and mysterious rapture during the summer of 1788.

Mozart's Final Symphonies

Mozart's popularity and finances suffered during the years surrounding the composing of these three symphonies: *Symphony No. 39 in E-flat, Symphony No. 40 in G minor*, and *Symphony No. 41 in C* (Jupiter).

Sophisticated listeners enjoyed his operas, especially *The Marriage of Figaro* and *Don Giovanni*. But to the listening public, his music was modern and difficult. He ranked seventh among the most popular opera composers of the time.

From 1788 on, war with the Ottoman Turks also engaged Austria. The population suffered under austerity measures, including the closing of the opera houses. Commissions and public performances that made up the bulk of Mozart's income fell off.

In the eight years since Mozart arrived in Vienna, his income had fallen almost in half. And yet despite his troubles, we have these three magnificent symphonies, the final two being awe-inspiring masterpieces.

What prompted Mozart to compose them?

No one knows.

The *Symphony No. 39 in E-flat*, a gentle and lyrical symphony, is often the third wheel of these three symphonies, a lighter symphony easily forgotten next to the titanic and intense ecstasies of the final two symphonies.

The first two movements of this symphony possess a pastoral quality reminiscent of Beethoven's magnificent *Symphony No. 6 in F*, nicknamed the "Pastoral":

Video 6: Beethoven: *Symphony No. 6 in F* (Pastoral, complete)

Every movement of Mozart's symphony is exquisite, but pay particular attention to the 2nd movement starting at 11:00. The final two movements shift into an exuberant yet simple mode:

Video 7: K. 543: *Symphony No. 39 in E-flat* (complete, Bohm)

00.00: *Adagio - Allegro*
09.07: *Andante con moto*
16.46: *Menuetto trio*
21.01: *Allegro*

Mozart composed *Symphony No. 39 in E-flat* on June 26, 1788. Four weeks later, on July 25, 1788, Mozart composed his *Symphony No. 40 in G minor*, a completely different world of musical composition, which we will explore in depth in the next chapter.

Robert Schumann called this symphony "nothing but lightness, grace, and charm," while Charles Rosen declared it to be "a work of passion, violence, and grief." Leonard Bernstein marvels that it is "a work of utmost passion utterly controlled, and of free chromaticism elegantly being contained."

Mozart's Symphony No. 40 in G minor
embodies a great mystery.

We will go deeper into this symphony in the next chapter. For now, listen to this version of the symphony with Leonard Bernstein conducting the Boston Symphony Orchestra. Although the 1st and 3rd movements are too slow here for my taste, but still a pace liked by many, Bernstein conducts the 2nd and 4th movements just right:

Video 8: K. 550: *Symphony No. 40 in G minor* (complete, Bernstein)

00.30: *Molto allegro*
09.00: *Andante*
17.15: *Menuetto - Allegretto - Trio*
22.20: *Finale. Allegro assai*

Mozart composed his final symphony, *Symphony No. 41 in C* (Jupiter), two weeks after composing *Symphony No. 40 in G minor* on August 10, 1788. During the final three-and-a-half years of his life, Mozart wrote no more symphonies, focusing his energy instead on his final three operas, various quartets and quintets, arias and other vocal music, as well as dances and minuets, and his unfinished *Requiem in D minor.*

Mozart's Jupiter symphony presents the listener with an extraordinary challenge in counterpoint: listening to several musical ideas at the same time and making sense of them. These separate musical lines show up mostly in the 1st and 4th movements.

Fortunately for us, Mozart goes to great lengths to keep his musical lines clear and coherent, so that many beginning listeners do not realize how much counterpoint is blended so seamlessly in his works.

The 1st movement establishes the movement's foundation in the first eight bars (the first six bars are shown in the image below). In the first four bars the middle C (the C nearest the center of the keys on the piano) forms the keystone of the musical arch. Here's what you see in the image of the sheet music's first two bars of the Violin I line:

[Bars 1 & 2]
C, followed by a rapid G-A-B-C, followed again by a rapid G-A-B-C

At the end of the second bar is the first of two Cs that lead into bars three and four:

[Bars 3 & 4]
C followed by three two-steps: C-B, D-C, G-F

Look closely at Bar 1 and you will see a lowercase "f" under all the notes. That "f" stands for *forte*, meaning *loud*. Now look at the end of Bar 2 and the beginning of Bar 3. You see under the notes at the bottom a lowercase *p*, which stands for *piano*, meaning *soft*. (A piano was originally called a *fortepiano* because compared to the harpsichord this new instrument could convey a full dynamic range of soft to loud. It was later shortened to *piano*.)

He repeats the opening four bars, but moves the notes a fifth higher. (The starting note for the first four bars is C. The starting note for the second four bars is G, four notes higher making it the fifth note.) So when you listen to the start of the 1st movement, you hear Mozart setting up a dynamic contrast between loud and soft notes.

What follows is hardly the kind of melodic flow we normally expect from Mozart. Instead, we get a strong, muscular movement of martial music announcing the arrival of something powerful and great. Then comes the melodic flow of a fresh second theme.

And the freshness continues throughout the movement:

Video 9: K. 551: *Symphony No. 41 in C* (Jupiter, I. Allegro Vivace, Mackerras)

The 2nd movement of No. 41 is one of the most beautiful Mozart ever composed. *Andante cantabile* means that the movement must be played in a slow singing style. No amount of analysis prepares you for its unearthly light and dark beauty, and chromatic strangeness (like when someone plays neighboring notes on a piano going up and down both white and black keys).

Listen for the haunting oboes:

Video 10: K. 551: *Symphony No. 41 in C* **(Jupiter, II. Andante Cantabile, Mackerras)**

The 5-minute 3rd movement is another heavily chromatic movement that has the most amazing set of falling notes. Listen how Mozart continually uses sets of four and five falling notes played off of the various instruments like leaves falling, being taken up again by the wind, only to fall once more.

Here is a perfect example of how a composer can take a simple idea and develop it into a sublime composition:

Video 11: K. 551: *Symphony No. 41 in C* **(Jupiter, III. Menuetto Allegretto, Mackerras)**

The final 4th movement is an amazing, rousing celebration.

I once sat in a car with a friend and played the final movement as the sun set in Monterey, California. The birds seem to fly with the music, the ocean waves were in tune with the rhythm. More amazingly, the sun winked below the horizon perfectly with the softened strings and horns that start at 10.24.

Music like this can seem to connect to heavenly experiences in this world, giving one the impression of universal coherence and meaning. The movement, in C major like the 1st movement, opens with four long notes C-D-F-E, which reappear throughout the movement in numerous ways.

Recall that the first movement started with four notes C-G-A-B, and in his remarkable way Mozart has, at the beginning and end, provided us with the complete octave C-D-E-F-G-A-B-C. Thus he brings one more example of the musical unity inherent in the Classical Style, which Mozart elevates to timeless art:

Video 12: K. 551: *Symphony No. 41 in C* **(Jupiter, IV. Molto Allegro, Mackerras)**

You may also wish to view a special video that presents the 4th movement in graphical form, which allows you to follow all of the instruments visually:

Video 13: K. 551: *Symphony No. 41 in C* **(Jupiter, IV. Molto Allegro, animated graph)**

Mozart's *Symphony No. 41 in C* must have astonished the Viennese audience of his day. Nothing would have prepared them for the complexity and intensity of this music. Mozart has left behind the music of his time and now foreshadows music that will not arrive until the next century.

According to Paul Johnson in his biography *Mozart*:

"Ludwig Wittgenstein [philosopher], who came from one of the most distinguished families in Vienna, used to say that No. 39 was for encouragement, No. 40 for second and third thoughts, and No. 41 for a glimpse of paradise, with reservations. 'The whole gamut of possible human emotions' is in these works, he believed."

In the next chapter, we delve into the mysteries of Mozart's *Symphony No. 40 in G minor*. We will discover how Mozart stayed within the classical form while simultaneously stretching his audience's hearing to the point that, even today, we would regard parts of this symphony as modern music.

Chapter 10

Hearing Mozart, Part 5:
Symphony No. 40 in G minor

"What a piece! No amount of analysis or explanation can prepare one for the overwhelming surprise of its existence when it is actually heard in performance. It is hard to think of another work that so perfectly marries form and passion."
Leonard Bernstein

Playlist 10: MarkAndreAlexander.com/One-Click-to-Mozart/
(15 videos, approx. 2 hrs 43 min)

In Western art we have a few stellar works that proclaim the worth of mankind: Egypt's Great Pyramid, Greece's Parthenon, Michelangelo's David, Shakespeare's plays, and Mozart's *Symphony No. 40 in G minor.*

1st Movement

Let's begin by listening to and viewing the 1st movement. As before, this special video uses an animated graph to help you "visually hear" the instruments, which are color-coded:

Video 1: K. 550: *Symphony No. 40 in G minor* (I. Allegro Molto, animated graph)

The opening motif of this symphony may seem familiar. Mozart introduced it briefly in the *Piano Concerto No. 21 in C* about four minutes into the 1st movement:

Video 2: K. 467: *Piano Concerto No. 21 in C* (opening)

This strong, intense movement stands as a model of passion and energy, tight and efficient, all with this use of strong chromaticism (using all twelve notes in an octave.) It foreshadows Beethoven in many ways, the simple motif, the strength, and the musical and thematic reflections among the instruments.

In fact, Beethoven copied out a portion of this symphony into his sketchbook while composing his famous *Symphony No. 5 in C minor*. Notice how Beethoven uses the simple four-note motif of his symphony in a way that's similar to Mozart's three-note motif:

Video 3: Beethoven: *Symphony No. 5 in C minor* (Kleiber)

Mozart appears to present a model of symmetry in his music. But that is not quite true. If Mozart were to be perfectly symmetric, he would be guilty of the charge "too many notes." Instead, within the symmetry Mozart begins deleting parts to come up with the final score.

Leonard Bernstein does a brilliant analysis of the opening of this movement in his second Norton lecture on "Musical Syntax." He focuses on symmetry and demonstrates what Mozart is actually doing.

You can get a flavor of how this symphony would sound if it *were* perfectly symmetrical, and how advanced musicians and conductors approach classical music by watching this video for seven minutes or so.

Even better, watch a full twenty minutes. It must have been nice to have an orchestra at your command to illustrate your musical examples. I've included only twenty minutes in the total time for this chapter's playlist:

Video 4: Leonard Bernstein: *The Unanswered Question, Part 2, Musical Syntax* (Symmetry)

Now listen again to the entire 1st movement, this time to what I believe is one of the most inspired performances. Sir Charles Mackerras includes all of Mozart's repeats and provides a brisk pace that is more in line with Mozart's metronome:

Video 5: K. 550: *Symphony No. 40 in G minor* (I. Allegro molto, Mackerras)

2nd Movement

This slower *Andante* at first sounds almost minimalistic. It's beautiful in its amazing simplicity, with subtle shadings and light two-note lilts. And still he inserts chromaticism throughout.

Again, Beethoven would have been impressed with how Mozart can make so much out of so little.

Many conductors remove some of Mozart's repeats. Sir Charles Mackerras wonderfully keeps them all:

Video 6: K. 550: *Symphony No. 40 in G minor* (II. Andante, Mackerras)

3rd Movement

This strident *menuetto* appears to continue Mozart's play with chromaticism, but there is hardly any chromaticism in it, except at the very end. What makes this movement so challenging is the beat. Mozart keeps shifting the downbeat.

To understand what this means, try using your hand to tap the beat on your knee. Where does each measure begin or end? In a sense, Mozart is playing a "chromatic" game with the beat, going off what's expected in order to present a challengingly new, yet classically contained, piece of music.

Many conductors play this movement slower, but when they do, they miss out on Mozart's intensity. Here is the intense version:

Video 7: K. 550: *Symphony No. 40 in G minor* (III. Menuetto - Allegro - Trio, Mackerras)

4th Movement

The 4th movement is one of Mozart's most radical. It must have tortured the ears of his contemporaries as both "too many notes" and "too dissonant."

Why?

Mozart exploits chromaticism in a way never heard before. He starts the development section with an atonal passage of eleven out of the twelve notes, eliminating the tonic note of G.

Leonard Bernstein declares,

*"What an inspired idea—all the notes except the tonic!
It could easily pass for twentieth-century music,
if we didn't already know it was Mozart."*

The 4th movement offers a dramatic example of sonata form. As a reminder, sonata form has four main parts: Exposition (often with two themes), Development, Recapitulation, and Coda. In this movement, however, Mozart eliminates the coda since it is not necessary.

Here's how the movement breaks down in our video example below:

00.00: Exposition, introducing two themes (repeated once).

03.36: Development, an extremely chromatic trip with lots of modulation between keys.

04:47: Recapitulation, returning to the first theme, but in a more truncated form; then Mozart repeats both the development and capitulation, bringing the entire movement to an end in such a way that no coda is necessary.

Unfortunately, YouTube does not currently offer a recording by Sir Charles Mackerras of the 4th movement. But this one is close:

Video 8: K. 550: *Symphony No. 40 in G minor* (IV. Allegro Assai)

Extended Discussion

Leonard Bernstein makes a strong case that Mozart's power of expression in the *Symphony No. 40 in G minor* arises from two oppositional forces: diatonicism and chromaticism. Shortly, I will have you watch a Leonard Bernstein video on the symphony, but to understand him, you need some technical background.

The diatonic scale is based on the *Circle of Fifths*, and Western *tonal* music is based on the stable relationship of these fifths, especially the *tonic* and *dominant* relationship.

What does all this mean? Here is a short tutorial on the circle of fifths. When the key is C major, the *tonic* is C-E-G. The *dominant* in relation to C is a *fifth* above: G-B-D.

The first five minutes of this video is all you need to start. (Watch the whole video if you find you're not getting confused):

Video 9: The Circle of Fifths: How to Actually Use It

Each fifth is a tonic/dominant relationship. C and G are a fifth apart and the chord C-E-G is very stable.

The circle of fifths is the foundation for diatonic, tonal music. Diatonicism is a force for tonal clarity.

So what is chromaticism and what difference does it make? Chromaticism introduces ambiguity and expressivity.

Here is a 2-minute video that clearly illustrates the difference between diatonicism and chromaticism, based on a Mozart variation:

Video 10: Diatonicism vs. Chromaticism

When you listen to the history of music from the Viennese Classical period through to today's Contemporary Classical, you hear more and more chromaticism until finally you lose almost all diatonicism. The result is *atonal* music.

This 2-minute video demonstrates the difference between tonal and atonal music:

Video 11: The Difference between Tonal and Atonal Music

Here is a famous atonal piece of music by the pioneering composer Arnold Schoenberg performed by famed pianist Glenn Gould:

Video 12: Schoenberg: *Three Piano Pieces No. 1*

OK. Now you're ready for Bernstein's argument that Mozart uses chromaticism in amazing ways to increase the power of expression while staying within the bounds of the Viennese Classical Style. The 1ˢᵗ movement is in G minor, so G is the tonic, and the fifth above, which is D, is the dominant:

Video 13: Bernstein on Mozart

If you would like to go a bit deeper, here is a 5-minute video where Bernstein explains the development of the tonic and dominant, leading to the circle of fifths, to the chromatic scale, and to the twelve keys of music:

Video 14: Bernstein, The Greatest 5 minutes in Musical Education

For readers interested in Bernstein's entire first lecture (of six) of his Norton Lectures at Harvard University, below is the link (the rest being located in the *Appendix: Online Music, Films, and Lectures*).

Bernstein assumes his audience has a background in classical rhetoric and in Noam Chomsky's transformational grammar (it being a Harvard audience, after all). I've included this in the playlist, but not counted it as part of the total time:

Video 15: Leonard Bernstein, *The Unanswered Question, Part 1, Musical Phonology* 1h 45m

I know it sometimes seems like studious work, watching these videos and trying to understand a new language. But like any kind of exercise, you build strengths and skills that grant you new capabilities.

Leonard Bernstein and these musical examples can help you build powerful musical muscles that give you access to states of musical consciousness that provide ongoing transcendent visions and experiences of sublime truth and beauty.

In the next chapter, we aim to help those unfamiliar with opera understand why so many music lovers love this special, and seemingly artificial, musical form. We tackle Mozart's operas by guiding you thoroughly through one of the best operas of all time.

Chapter 11

Mozart and Opera:
Le nozze di Figaro (The Marriage of Figaro)

*"Designing an opera by Mozart is like
doing something for God—
it's a labor of love."*
Maurice Sendak

Playlist 11: MarkAndreAlexander.com/One-Click-to-Mozart/
(18 videos, 6 hrs 13 min)

**Mozart loved opera above all other music and aspired to be a
great opera composer.**

He loved the fusion of music, stage, song, and story. Opera allowed him to express more of the range of the human emotions he had experienced, as well as to explore the depths of human relationships.

> *Opera allowed Mozart to easily accomplish in the musical world what he could not adequately manage in the daily human world.*

But to his great frustration, he received few commissions for operas in Vienna. However, those few commissions set a standard rarely equaled and never surpassed for the two main opera forms: *Opera buffa* (comic) and *Opera seria* (serious).

To the novice, opera can appear to be silly and artificial. Certainly it has been easy to caricature, especially by Bugs Bunny:

Video 1: Bugs Bunny: What's Opera Doc?

Add to that, in Mozart's day, in between songs, all dialogue was sung in a *recitative* style that resembles speech. And the singing involved a lot of repetition, so that even a long song could have simple lyrics.

Opera enacts the musical and vocal drama or comedy of a story, with heightened meaning and emotions. Mozart loved Shakespeare, but as a composer he took his love of stage and story, sought out *librettists* (lyric writers who would supply the opera composer with the lyrics to the story), and brought to the opera stage some of the most exquisite opera the world has ever seen.

Many musicians, aristocrats, and critics of Mozart's time failed to fully appreciate Mozart's music, especially his operas. Shortly after his death, a critic in the 1793 German periodical, "Journal de Luxus under der Moden" wrote:

"Mozart's talent appears to be an original one, which nevertheless tends towards affectation, towards bizarre, surprising and paradoxical passages, both melodic and harmonic, and avoids the natural flow so as not to become ordinary...His melody is overburdened with too many harmonic changes, accompaniments, and difficult striking intervals which are often hard for the singer to intone and remember...a genius who worked according to a plan in which one cannot sanction the hard modulations, improper imitations, and intricate accompaniments."

Around 1799, Italian opera composer Giuseppe Sarti composed the opera *Fra i due litiganti il terzo gode*, which greatly influenced Mozart's own *Le nozze di Figaro*. Sarti wrote:

"The composer, whom I do not know and do not want to know, is a clavier [piano] player with a depraved ear; he follows that false system which divides the octave into semitones...music to make you block your ears."

Perhaps like many today, they thought Mozart's operas trivial or superficial. Nothing could be further from the truth. In fact, during the nineteenth century, many musicians and aristocrats thought Mozart too simple, and would agree with Sir Hubert Parry's assessment in 1890: "Mozart was not naturally a man of deep feeling or intellectuality, and the result is that his variation building is neither impressive nor genuinely interesting."

Of course, Mozart's music is the opposite of simple.

"Mozart's music is particularly difficult to perform.
His admirable clarity exacts absolute cleanness:
the slightest mistake in it stands out like black on white.
It is music in which all the notes must be heard."
Gabriel Faure, composer

"The works of Mozart may be easy to read,
but they are very difficult to interpret.
The least speck of dust spoils them.
They are clear, transparent, and joyful as a spring,
and not like those muddy pools which seem deep
only because the bottom cannot be reached."
Wanda Landowska, harpsichordist

We have space to cover one opera in depth. But it is worthwhile to listen to Mozart's seven great opera overtures, in order, as previews of coming attractions.

Listen for the love and brilliance that comes through all of them. I have added some quotes to introduce each overture:

"In Idomeneo Mozart, abruptly, comes of age.
True there had been a steady deepening of
his musical style in the years leading up to it...
Yet nothing prepares for the explosion of Idomeneo.
David Cairns, British musical journalist

Video 2: K. 366: *Idomeneo, re di Creta (Idomeneo, King of Crete), Overture*

* * *

"...The Abduction from the Seraglio,
an exotic piece with a Turkish theme.
In less than a year, the opera would open
to the most enthusiastic reception
Mozart was to get for an opera until
The Magic Flute was performed, ten years later."
Robert Harris, English music critic

Video 3: K. 384: *Die Entführung aus dem Serail (The Abduction from the Seraglio), Overture*

* * *

"That is the most beautiful overture in the world."
Franz Schubert, after hearing the overture to *Le nozze di Figaro*

Video 4: K. 492: *Le nozze di Figaro (The Marriage of Figaro,* **Overture**

* * *

*"By almost universal agreement,
Figaro and [Don] Giovanni are Mozart's two best operas."*
Paul Johnson, Mozart biographer

Video 5: K. 527: *Don Giovanni,* **Overture**

* * *

*"...without a doubt, the most personal and autobiographical
of all of Mozart's twenty-two operas...an opera about wife-
swapping and the supposed 'inconstancy' of women."*
Robert Greenberg,American composer and teacher

Video 6: K. 588: *Cosi Fan Tutte (Thus Do They All),*
Overture

* * *

*"The mock-solemn overture to
Die Zauberflöte is one of the most brilliant
instrumental movements Mozart ever fashioned."*
Ted Libby, NPR music critic

Video 7: K. 620: *The Magic Flute* **(Overture)**

* * *

*"In the decade after Mozart's death,
['La Clemenza di Tito'] became a symbol
of his noblest work and was frequently performed."*
Nicholas Kenyon, British director of the BBC Proms

Video 8: K. 621: *La Clemenza di Tito (The Clemency of Titus)*

The Marriage of Figaro

Le nozze di Figaro is widely regarded as not only Mozart's greatest *opera buffa* but also the greatest *opera buffa* of all time.

This special section is designed for you to watch the four acts of this great opera as you review a summary of the action in each scene.

Be sure to pause at those points to read more as you move from scene-to-scene.

***

ACT I
Video 9: K. 492: *Le nozze di Figaro, Act I* **(Carlo Maria Giulini)**

Act I has four *Arias* (Solos), four *Duettinos* (Duets), two *Cavitinas* (Little Solos), two *Coros* (Chorus of Singers), and one *Terzetto* (Trio).

Overture

Scene 1

The setting is 18th century Spain on the wedding day of Figaro and Susanna, servants to Count Almaviva. Figaro is measuring out the wedding bed. He learns from his fiancé that the Count intends to claim his right as feudal lord to sleep with new brides. This is the opera's first *Duettino*, "*Cinque... dieci... venti...*" Susanna then leaves.

Scene 2

Alone with his anger, Figaro vows to school the Count by coming up with a cunning plan to stop him. He sings the opera's first *Cavatina*, "*Se vuol ballare, signor Contino.*" Figaro then leaves.

Scene 3

The lawyer Dr. Bartolo enters with Marcellina, his old housekeeper. She has hired him to enforce Figaro's promise to marry her if he should default on paying back money she loaned to him. Dr. Bartolo also seeks revenge for Figaro stealing away his love, Susanna. Bartolo sings the opera's first *Aria*, "*La Vendetta, oh, la vendetta.*" He leaves.

Scene 4

Susanna enters, and she and Marcellina exchange polite but sarcastic insults. They sing the opera's second *Duettino*, "*Via resti servita, madama brillante.*" Marcellina then leaves.

Scene 5

Cherubino, the pageboy, arrives frustrated because the Count found him with Barbarina and dismissed him. (A female actor sometimes performs this role.) He asks for Susanna's help to punish him. To reward her, Cherubino gives her a song he wrote, and sings the opera's second *Aria*, "*Non so più cosa son, cosa faccio.*"

Scene 6

The Count arrives and, while Cherubino hides behind a chair, demands favors from Susanna, even asking her to sell herself to him. A creepy music teacher named Basilio then announces his arrival, and the Count hides behind the same chair. Just in time, Cherubino jumps onto the chair and Susanna quickly covers him with a dress.

Scene 7

Basilio enters and gossips about Cherubino's attraction to the Countess. The Count leaps up, denouncing his page and describing how he caught him with Barbarina. They sing the opera's first *Terzetto*, "*Susanna, or via, sortite.*"

The Count lifts Susanna's dress from the chair to illustrate how he lifted the tablecloth to find Cherubino, and exposes Cherubino again. Susanna reminds the Count how Cherubino has overheard his attempts to seduce Susanna.

Scene 8

Villagers enter the Count's estate, a preemptive attempt by Figaro to commit the Count to a formal gesture symbolizing his promise that Susanna would enter into the marriage without submitting to the Count's seduction. They sing the opera's first *Coro*, "*Giovani lieti.*"

The Count postpones the gesture, forgives Cherubino, and dispatches him to his own regiment in Seville for army duty. Then, Figaro mocks Cherubino on his new military life that excludes women, singing the famous *Aria*, "*Non piu andrai.*" The Act ends.

***

ACT II
Video 10: K. 492: *Le nozze di Figaro, Act II* (Carlo Maria Giulini)

Act II has one *Aria,* one *Arietta* (Shorter *Aria*), one *Duettino,* one *Cavitina,* one *Terzetto,* and three *Finales.*

Scene 1:

Knowing the Count's plan to seduce Susanna, the solitary Countess sings her pain. *Cavatina*, *"Porgi, amor."*

Scene 2:

Susanna enters and the Countess confirms her account. Then Figaro enters and since he knows of the Count's plans to help Marcellina, Figaro's plan is to have Basilio send the Count an anonymous note informing him that the Countess has a lover. Susanna will agree to meet the Count in the garden, and Cherubino will be disguised as Susanna. The Countess will then surprise them. Figaro leaves to find Cherubino.

Scene 3:

Cheurbino enters and Susanna asks him to sing the Countess a love song. *Arietta*, *"Voi che sapate."* Susanna starts dressing him as a woman and sings. *Aria*, *"Venite...inginocchiatevi...."* She goes off to another room to get a ribbon, and Cherubino tries to declare his love for the Countess.

Scene 4:

The Count knocks at the door and Cherubino hides in a closet.

Scene 5:

The Count enters and asks the Countess who she was speaking with, and she replies it was Susanna who is in another room. He shows her the anonymous note. There's a noise from the closet and the Countess now tells the Count that Susanna is in the closet.

Scene 6:

> Susanna enters unseen, and noticing there's a problem, hides behind a screen. The three sing, with Susanna singing to the side. *Terzetto*, *"Susanna, or via, sortite."* The Count, certain the Countess is hiding her lover, calls for "Susanna" to come out of the closet, but the Countess says no. The Count then takes her out with him to get something to break the closet open, locking the door.

Scene 7:

> Susanna lets Cherubino out of the closet, and they sing a *Duettino*, *"Aprite, presto, aprite."* He escapes through the window. It's now Susanna's turn to hide in the closet.

Scene 8:

> When they return, the Countess reveals that Cherubino is in the closet, claiming it was a joke. The Count threatens to kill Cherubino and draws his sword.

Scene 9:

> He opens the closet and they are both amazed to find Susanna. The three begin singing the first *Finale*, *"Esci, ormai, garson mainato."* The Count begs his wife's forgiveness. The Countess and Susanna explain how the anonymous note was just a prank. The Count, and they reconcile.

Scene 10:

> The second *Finale*, *"Signore, di fuori,"* begins as Figaro arrives to say the wedding will start shortly. The Count asks him about the prank, and he denies writing the note or sending Cherubino. The Count seizes the opportunity to stop the wedding between Figaro and Suzanna.

Scene 11:

The gardener, Antonio, runs in saying that someone has jumped from the Countess's balcony into his flower garden. Having seen Cherubino jump, Figaro claims that he himself was the one who jumped. But the gardener says he saw a boy, and the Count knows it was Cherubino.

Figaro stays with his story, and says that Cherubino was on his way to Seville. Figaro says he himself hid in the closet waiting for Susanna, but then overheard the Count shouting and chose to escape by jumping. He claims he hurt his foot and suddenly develops a limp.

The gardener shows the Count a military commission he found in the garden. The gardener leaves. The Countess informs Susanna, who then informs Figaro that it's Cherubino's commission. Figaro then explains that Cherubino gave it to him because it lacks a seal.

Scene 12:

The third *Finale*, "*Voi signor, che giusto siete*," begins with the arrival of Marcellina, Bartolo, and Basilio, who want justice. They explain to the Count that Figaro entered into a contract to marry Marcellina in exchange for a loan. The Count agrees to decide the case.

***

ACT III
Video 11: K. 492: *Le nozze di Figaro, Act III* (Carlo Maria Giulini)

Act III has one *Sestetto* (a sextet, six singers), one *Coro*, one *Arias*, two Duettinos, and one *Finale*.

Scene 1:

> Alone, the Count thinks about the events that have happened. He decides that he cannot insult the Countess by doubting her.

Scene 2:

> Unseen, the Countess urges Susanna to ask the Count to meet her later in the garden. Since Cherubino is not available, the Countess decides to impersonate Susanna.
>
> The Countess leaves, and Susanna overhears the Count talking about Figaro and Marcellina. She walks up to him saying she needs smelling salts for the Countess, who has fainted.
>
> The Count replies that she will need the smelling salts for herself, since she will lose her fiancé, Figaro. She says she will repay Marcellina's loan with the dowry promised by the Count, but the Count says he never made such a promise. Susanna flirts with him, and they sing a *Duettino*, "*Crudel! perchè finora.*" They make a deal.

Scene 3:

> As Susanna leaves, she sees Figaro, and the Count overhears her telling Figaro that they've "won the case."

Scene 4:

> The angry Count plans to punish them. He sings the *Aria*, "*Hai già vinta la causa*" and leaves.

Scene 5:

> Barbarina and Cherubino enter. She wants Cherubino to stay in the castle and convinces him to dress like a girl at her home. They leave.

Scene 6:

The Countess enters, wondering whether the plan to catch the Count's infidelity will succeed. She's unhappy at the loss of their love, and as she leaves, she hopes to regain his love. She sings the beautiful Aria, "*Dove sono i beimomenti*" and leaves.

Scene 7:

A judge, Don Curzio, arrives with Marcellina and Bartolo, and states that Figaro must either repay the loan or marry Marcellina. Figaro claims noble birth and that he cannot marry without the approval of his relatives. The Count asks who these noble relatives are, and Figaro responds that thieves stole him as an infant. He plans to find his parents in ten years.

Bartolo asks for proof. Figaro shows him a birthmark on his arm that reveals that he is a bastard of Marcellina and Bartolo! All six sing the Sestetto, "*Riconosci in questo amplesso*." The reunited family hugs.

Susanna enters with enough money to pay off Marcellina, only to be upset seeing Figaro and Marcellina embrace. Figaro explains that Marcellina is his mother and Bartolo his father. All goodwill is restored, and the Count flees with Don Curzio.

Scene 8:

Bartolo proposes to Marcellina, who then tears up Figaro's loan. Bartolo provides Figaro and Susanna with a dowry, and Susanna adds to it the money she brought. They all laugh at the Count's frustration, and leave to plan a double wedding.

Scene 9:

The Count arrives with the gardener, who tells the Count that Cherubino is still in the neighborhood, because he found the woman's clothes that Cherubino had worn. They go to find him.

Scene 10:

The Countess and Susanna enter, and create a note from Susanna to the Count requesting a meeting in the garden. Here begins one of the loveliest songs in all opera, the one we heard from the film *The Shawshank Redemption*, the justly famous *Duettino*, "*Canzonetta sull'aria 'Che soave seffiretto.'*"

Here are the lyrics in Italian and English:

Susanna: Sull'aria...   (On the breeze...)
Contessa: Che souve zeffiretto... (What a gentle little Zephyr...)
Susanna: Zeffiretto... (A little Zephyr...)
Contessa: Questa sera spirerà... (This evening will sigh...)
Susanna: Questa sera spirerà... (This evening will sigh...)
Contessa: Sotto i pini del boschetto. (Under the pines in the little grove.)
Susanna: Sotto i pini... (Under the pines...)
Contessa: Sotto i pini del boschetto. (Under the pines in the little grove...)
Susanna: Sotto i pini del boschetto. (Under the pines in the little grove...)
Contessa: Ei già il resto capirà. (And the rest he'll understand.)
Both: Certo, certo il capirà. (Certainly, certainly he'll understand.)
Both: [They reread what has been written.]

The Countess and Susanna seal the note with a pin for the Count to return once he agrees to meet.

[Notice that Bernard Haitink conducts this song more briskly than the version from *The Shawshank Redemption*. His conducting emphasizes the playful and mischievous nature of their plan to fool the Count. In the process, the song loses some of its sonorous beauty. This difference demonstrates how much the conductor can influence how the music is shaped, and what meaning it conveys.]

Scene 11:

Barbarina and some peasant girls, who include the disguised Cherubino, arrive to serenade the Countess with the *Coro*, "*Ricevete, o padroncina.*"

Scene 12:

The gardener and the Count arrive. The Count unmasks Cherubino and threatens to punish him. But Barbarina persuades the Count, who once promised her anything after kissing her, to let her marry Cherubino. The Count is embarrassed in front of the Countess.

Scene 13:

Figaro arrives and the Count questions him again. The gardener reveals Cherubino as proof that Figaro lied. But Figaro says it's possible that both of them jumped into the garden. As a wedding march begins, so does the *Finale*, "*Ecco la marcia...andiamo.*"

Everyone leaves to get ready, and the Count and Countess are now alone. She refuses to talk to him.

Scene 14:

The *Finale* continues. The wedding party returns in
procession, and while they sing of abolishing the Count's
feudal right to sleep with the bride, Susanna slips him the
sealed note. As the couples dance, the Count reads the
note and pricks his finger on the pin, which he drops.
Figaro watches with humor, believing it to be some kind
of love note. The Count retrieves the pin, excited at the
thought of meeting with Susanna in the garden, and
invites everyone to a wedding banquet.

***

ACT IV
**Video 12: K. 492: *Le nozze di Figaro, Act IV* (Carlo Maria
Giulini)**

Act IV has one *Cavitina*, four *Arias,* and three *Finales.*

Scene 1:

Upset, Barbarina searches the garden for something lost.
She sings the *Cavatina*, *"L'ho perduta...me meschina!"*

Scene 2:

Figaro arrives with Marcellina and asks Barbarina what's
wrong. She says that she has lost the pin that the Count
gave her to deliver to Susanna as a token of their
agreement. Figaro pretends that he already knows about
it, and plucks a pin from Marcellina's dress, giving it to
Barbarina, who goes off to give it to Susanna.

Scene 3:

Figaro falls into his mother's arms, upset because he
believes Susanna is betraying him. She advises that he

stay calm, but anger overtakes him and he exits, vowing to avenge all deceived husbands.

Scene 4:

Marcellina, afraid for Susanna, sings of her concern in the *Aria*, "*Il capro e la capretta.*" She goes off to warn her.

Scene 5:

Barbarina enters with fruit and looks at the left pavilion where she had arranged to meet Cherubino. She wonders if he will come as promised. She hears someone coming and flees into the pavilion.

Scene 6:

Figaro enters with Basilio and Bartolo to requests they aid him in helping him trap Susanna and the Count. He leaves.

Scene 7:

Basilio and Bartolo talk about Figaro's desire to clash with important people. Basilio sings the *Aria*, "*In quegli anni in cui vai poco,*" in which he tells a story that taught him the value of hiding beneath an ass's skin to avoid shame, humiliation, and death.

Scene 8:

Figaro enters and denounces the perfidy of women in the *Aria*, "*Aprite un po' quegli occhi.*"

Scene 9:

Figaro hides as Susanna and Marcellina enter, both in disguise, with the Countess. Marcellina warns Susanna that Figaro is already in the garden. That suits Susanna just fine, as she can avenge herself on both Figaro for his jealousy and the Count for his philandering. Marcellina hides in the pavilion.

Scene 10:

The nervous Countess hides while Susanna stays to enjoy the breeze. To punish the spying Figaro, Susanna sings the *Aria*, "*Deh, vieni, non tardar, o gioia bella.*" She then hides, putting on the Countess's cloak.

Scene 11:

Though Figaro is irate, he continues to hide as Cherubino enters looking for Barbarina. The Countess also enters, disguised as Susanna. Cherubino begins flirting with her, thinking she's Susanna. Here begins the *First Finale*, "*Pian pianin le andrò più presso.*"

The Count arrives and receives the kiss meant for "Susanna." The Count tries to slap Cherubino but Figaro enters and receives the slap while Cherubino runs off.

Now the Count, believing they're alone, begins flirting with "Susanna," angering Figaro even more. The Count tries to lure her into the dark pavilion, but he then hears Figaro's voice and fears discovery. He instructs "Susanna" to go ahead into the pavilion without him. He exits, promising to meet her later.

Figaro emerges and the *Second Finale* begins, "*Tutto è tranquillo e placido.*" The real Susanna arrives, disguised as the Countess. Hearing her voice, Figaro immediately realizes that she is the real Susanna. As a joke, he pretends to court "the Countess." Now it's Susanna's turn to be furious. Finally, Figaro reveals his joke, and they tenderly reconcile. But then the Count returns, so the couple decides to replay the joke for the Count.

Scene 12:

Now begins the *Third Finale, "Gente, gente, all'armi."*
The angry Count grabs Figaro and calls for weapons.
Susanna flees into the pavilion. At that point, Bartolo,
Basilio, Antonio, and Curzio enter. The Count calls for
his wife to come out of the pavilion.

To everyone's surprise, out come Cherubino, Barbarina,
Marcellina, and Susanna, still dressed as the Countess.
Susanna and Figaro pretend to beg the Count's
forgiveness. The Count refuses them, but then the real
Countess reveals herself.

The chastened and humbled Count begs the pardon of
the Countess. She grants it, and everyone rejoices. The
opera ends.

***

Famed English writer Virginia Woolf, after seeing this opera
in 1917, wrote:

"It's perfectly lovely, breaking from one beauty into
another, and so Romantic as well as witty—the
perfection of music, and the vindication of opera.

When you are ready for more of Mozart's operas, the next
section provides some online recommendations.

Extended Discussion

Here are some fine video recordings of Mozart's other six
great operas, some with no subtitles or subtitles in languages
other than English.

Idomeneo, re di Creta (Idomeneo, King of Crete)

Video 13: **K. 366: *Idomeneo, re di Creta* (full video)**

Die Entführung aus dem Serail (The Abduction from the Seraglio)

Video 14: **K. 384: *The Abduction from the Seraglio* (full video)**

Don Giovanni (Don Juan)

Video 15: K. 527: *Don Giovanni* (full video)

Cosi Fan Tutte (Thus Do They All)

Video 16: K. 588: *Cosi Fan Tutte* (full video)

Die Zauberflöte (The Magic Flute)

Video 17: K. 620: *The Magic Flute* (full video)

La Clemenza di Tito (The Clemency of Titus)

Video 18: K. 621: La clemenza di Tito (full video)

Chapter 12

Mozart's Heavenly Mansion

"Mozart, like Shakespeare, continues to grow.
His music is an ever-expanding universe.
The better we know it—the more we explore its
heights and depths—the more marvellous it becomes."
David Cairns

Playlist 12: MarkAndreAlexander.com/One-Click-to-Mozart/
(17 videos, 2 hrs 12 min)

Mozart's music is singularly inspired.

"Mozart in his music was probably
the most reasonable of the world's great composers.
It is the happy balance between flight and control, between
sensibility and self-discipline, simplicity and
sophistication of style that is his particular province...
Mozart tapped once again the source from which
all music flows, expressing himself with a spontaneity
and refinement and breath-taking rightness
that has never since been duplicated."
Aaron Copland, composer

"He roused my admiration when I was young;
he caused me to despair when I reached maturity;
he is now the comfort of my old age."
Gioachino Rossini, composer

"Before Mozart, all ambition turns to despair."
Charles Gounod, composer

"Mozart is sunshine."
Antonin Dvorak, composer

If you have any doubt that meaning can be conveyed musically, or vocally even without knowing the words, the selections in this final chapter may convince you.

Some of these you have heard before. Many are drawn from my list of twelve singularly inspired recordings on CD that every home library should have. (See "Recommended Readings and Recordings.")

As you listen to these excerpts
one after the other,
you will notice a certain
cumulative effect within you.

Set aside the time to read this entire chapter and listen to the excerpts in order in a single sitting. Turn off your phone. Once you start, don't stop.

Mozart wrote many serenades. A serenade is small chamber orchestral music for upper-class households. Serenades are often composed in honor of someone, and are often played in the open air at night.

Serenades are meant to be light, calming, and in the slower movements, serene. We start with two of the best, including one that is for woodwinds (two oboes, two clarinets, two horns, and two bassoons):

Video 1: K. 250: *Serenade No. 7 in D, Haffner* **(II. Andante)**

Video 2: K. 375: *Serenade No. 11 in E-flat for Winds* **(III. Adagio)**

You may recall that we examined the 3rd movement of Mozart's *Serenade No. 10 in B-flat for Winds*. But the 6th movement has a heavenly surprise in the last third of the movement. Wait for the serene beauty of the winds about six minutes in:

Video 3: K. 361: *Serenade No. 10 in B-flat for Winds* **(VI. Tema con variazioni)**

Thank heavens the clarinet arrived on the musical scene in time for Mozart to write music for it. Let's once again listen to the heavenly 2nd movement of the *Clarinet Concerto in A*:

Video 4: K. 622: *Clarinet Concerto in A* **(II. Adagio, Shifrin)**

Mozart not only wrote serenades for small chamber orchestras; he also wrote *divertimentos*, which were meant to be lighthearted music for social functions. Yet even in these, Mozart cannot help but write profound and deeply touching music:

Video 5: K. 138: *Divertimento in F* **(II. Andante)**

Try to imagine Mozart's interior musical landscape while composing. Imagine his inner musical home.

Did his inner state come forth in his music?

Some say no because of the example of the three great symphonies of 1788.

But let's assume that it did reflect his inner state. What does that mean?

Let's listen again to the 2nd movement of Mozart's *Symphony No. 41 in G minor*:

Video 6: K. 551: *Symphony No. 41 in C* (Jupiter, II. Andante Cantabile, Mackerras)

The slow movements of Mozart's piano concertos hold a special place in the heart. Here is a series of just the 2nd movements of several of those concertos:

Video 7: K. 414: *Piano Concerto No. 12 in A* (II. Andante, Ashkenazy)

Video 8: K. 466: *Piano Concerto No. 20 in D minor* (II. Romanze, Uchida)

Video 9: K. 467: *Piano Concerto No. 21 in C* (II. Andante, Brendel)

Video 10: K. 488: *Piano Concerto No. 23 in A* (II. Adagio, Gulda)

Video 11: K. 491: *Piano Concerto No. 24 in C minor* (II. Larghetto, Brendel)

Video 12: K. 537: *Piano Concerto No. 26 in D* (II. Larghetto, Klien)

Imagine living daily with this kind of music in your head. Imagine the ability, not only to hear an entire orchestra in your mind's ear, but also being in the midst of composing it.

Imagine the musical voices in your head.

Here is a famous *aria* from *Don Giovanni*, "*Vedrai carino*." What is she singing? Does it matter?

Video 13: K. 527: *Don Giovanni, aria "Vedrai carino"* (Bartoli)

Listen again to that famous duet, played twice, from *Le nozze di Figaro*. Here again are the lyrics in Italian (and English):

Susanna:	Sull'aria... (On the breeze...)
Contessa:	Che souve zeffiretto... (What a gentle little Zephyr...)
Susanna:	Zeffiretto... (A little Zephyr...)
Contessa:	Questa sera spirerà... (This evening will sigh...)
Susanna:	Questa sera spirerà... (This evening will sigh...)
Contessa:	Sotto i pini del boschetto. (Under the pines in the little grove.)
Susanna:	Sotto i pini... (Under the pines...)
Contessa:	Sotto i pini del boschetto. (Under the pines in the little grove...)
Susanna:	Sotto i pini del boschetto. (Under the pines in the little grove...)
Contessa:	Ei già il resto capirà. (And the rest he'll understand.)
Both:	Certo, certo il capirà. (Certainly, certainly he'll understand.)
Both:	[They reread what has been written.]

Video 14: K. 492: "Duettino Sull'aria" from *Le nozze di Figaro (The Marriage of Figaro)*

Next is the *"Et incarnatus est"* from Mozart's *Great Mass in C minor*, the piece that Pope Francis declared to be "matchless; it lofts you to God!" It was composed in 1783 for his new bride, Constanze:

Video 15: K. 427: *Great Mass in C minor, "Et incarnatus est"*

In the two years prior to composing the next piece of music in 1780, Mozart's marriage proposal was rejected, his attempt in Paris to win a position failed, and his mother died.

Perhaps that suffering set the stage for this amazing Catholic music. But you don't need to be a Catholic to be moved by such stunning beauty. The vocalist is Kiri Te Kanawa:

Video 16: K. 339: *Vesperae solennes de confessore* (V. Laudate dominum omnes gentes Kiri Te Kanawa

Is there any doubt that Mozart had direct access to a heavenly state of musical consciousness?

Mozart died without the patronage he deserved. However, the greatest composer in his lifetime, the great Franz Joseph Haydn, did recognize Mozart's gifts and lamented his lack of patronage.

In 1787, less than three years before Mozart's death, he spoke then, and does now, for all true lovers of Mozart:

> "I only wish I could impress on every friend of mine, and on great men in particular, the same depth of musical sympathy and profound appreciation of Mozart's inimitable music that I myself feel and enjoy; then nations would vie with each other to possess such a jewel within their frontiers.... It enrages me to think that the unparalleled Mozart is not yet engaged by some imperial or royal court! Forgive my excitement, but I love the man so dearly!"

Frederic Chopin's last request before he died was... "Play Mozart for me!"

Gustav Mahler's last word before he passed away was... "Mozart!"

In *Creating Your Life (A Lifetime of Learning, Book 1)*, I told the story about how in the space of six months I learned to conduct a choir before thousands of people. One of the three pieces we performed was a variant with English lyrics of one of

Mozart's final compositions—the serene and heavenly *Ave Verum Corpus.*

It is well worth setting on repeat and contemplating to this great music. Despite its Latin lyrics, *Ave Verum Corpus* has a way of working into a place deeper than your heart:

Video 17: K. 618: *Ave verum corpus* (Leonard Bernstein)

For me, more than any other piece of music, this brief, sacred, transcendent music sums up Mozart's transformation into a heavenly home.

And so we are now at the end, or more accurately, the beginning. For as you can see, there is a lifetime of musical works to explore—not just Mozart's, but those of all the other great composers that somehow touch the sublime and take us into heaven.

To start, go to the One-Click-To-Mozart page on my website. There, you can find links to almost every single work of the hundreds by Mozart.

But let us not forget the one dear soul who welcomes them all, for he resides there, with a room all to himself.

May we all visit Mozart there, now,
in his room, all by himself, and then again
when we finally release the burdens of this world.

The *Mozart and Great Music* Checklist

"I have always reckoned myself among
the greatest admirers of Mozart,
and shall remain so until my last breath."
Ludwig van Beethoven

Recognize that Great Art:

__Is objectively great, not a matter of subjective opinion.

__Transports one into realms that makes one wonder, "How is it possible that a mere human being created that?"

__Can imbue a spiritual revelation each time one experiences it.

__Carves out states of consciousness that transcend the human.

__Embodies an eternal mystery.

__Catalyzes, transforms, and transfigures.

Listen to Mozart:

__Actually listen to the recommended examples while working through the book.

__Acquire the recommended music and listen to it in full stereo.

__Watch operas, understanding that, like all great art, you must invest time and repetition to experience the deeper wonders.

__When possible, attend live performances; you will be astonished at how different they can be.

__Listen to Mozart daily and watch how, over time, you find less tension stress in your life.

Study Mozart and His Music:

__Read the first three texts in "Recommended Readings and Recordings."

__Get Robert Greenberg's *Great Courses*, especially *Great Masters: Mozart—His Life and Music*, and *The Operas of Mozart*.

__Watch the film *Amadeus*.

__Watch the BBC productions of "The Genius of Mozart," referred to in "Videos About Mozart and Great Music" located in the Appendix.

__Take the time to work through Leonard Bernstein complete Norton Lectures on *The Unanswered Question* referred to in "Videos About Mozart and Great Music" located in the Appendix.

Share Mozart with Family and Friends

__Find the music of Mozart that you most love and share.

__Surprise someone with a date to watch a live concert of Mozart's music.

Recommended Readings and Recordings

TEXTS

Cairns, David. (2006.) *Mozart and his Operas.* New York: Penguin.

Harris, Robert. (1991.) *What to Listen for in Mozart.* New York: Simon & Schuster.

> A short, mid-level work that combines biography with analysis of key Mozart compositions. Provides a nice introduction to reading musical scores (without needing to understand the different notes).

Johnson, Paul. (2013.) *Mozart.* New York: Viking Penguin. A shorter, easy-to-read biography.

Kenyon, Nicholas. (2006.) *The Pegasus Pocket Guide to Mozart.* New York: Pegasus Books.

Rosen, Charles. (1997.) *The Classical Style: Haydn, Mozart Beethoven.* New York: W.W. Norton & Company. A more serious and scholarly study of the Viennese classical style. Dense, detailed, thoughtful, and rich.

Solomon, Maynard. (1995.) *Mozart: A Life.* New York: HarperCollins Publishers. A longer, scholarly biography.

* * *

RECORDING GUIDES

Svejda, Jim. (1999.) *The Insider's Guide to Classical Recordings. Sixth edition.* Roseville, CA: Prima Publishing. This is my favorite A to Z recording guide, even though some of the recommendations are outdated. Jim is idiosyncratic, sharp, and opinionated. Of the 811 pages, 40 pages focus on Mozart, more than twice any other composer. Jim Svejda says, "Were this book to do him any justice, the section devoted to Mozart's music would take up more than half of this total book."

Swafford, Jim. (1992.) *The Vintage Guide to Classical Music.* New York: Vintage Books.

Libby, Ted. (1999.) *The NPR Guide to Building a Classical CD Collection.* Second edition. New York: Workman Publishing Company.

* * *

MUSICAL CD RECORDINGS

Generally speaking, the best conductors and performers create inspired performances. Occasionally, one particular performance of a work stands out among the rest.

Conductors I personally recommend for Mozart symphonies, serenades, and divertimentos include Sir Neville Marriner, Sir Charles Mackerras, Leonard Bernstein, and Sir Colin Davis.

For piano concertos and sonatas, the standout pianists are Alfred Brendel, Murray Perahia, Geza Anda, and Mitsuko Uchida.

What follows is a starter set of twelve singularly inspired recordings on CD that every home library should have:

1. Mozart Overtures: K. 135, K. 366, K. 384, K. 486, K. 492, K. 527, K. 588, K. 620, K. 621
    Neville Marriner, conductor; Academy of St. Martin-in-the-Fields (EMI Classics 7470142)

2. Concerto for Piano and Orchestra No. 21 in C major K. 467, Concerto for Piano and Orchestra No. 26 in D major K. 537, 12 Variations on "Ah, vous dirai-je, Maman" in C major K. 265
Robert Casadesus, piano; George Szell, conductor (Sony SBK 67178)

3. K. 622: Clarinet Concerto in A major , and K. 581: Clarinet Quintet in A major
David Shifrin, Clarinet; Gerard Schwarz, conductor (Delos DE 3020)

4. K. 339: Vesperae solennes de confessore; K. 341: Kyrie in D minor; K. 618: Ave verum corpus; and K. 165: Exsultate Jubilate .
Kiri Te Kanawa; Sir Colin Davis, conductor (Philips 4128732)

5. K. 364: Sinfonia Concertante, and K. 190: Concertone
Itzhak Perlman, violin; Pinchas Zuckerman, viola (Deutsche Grammophon 4154862)

6. K. 550: Symphony No. 40 in G minor, and K. 551 Symphony No. 41 in C major (Jupiter)
Sir Charles Mackerras, conductor (TELARC CD-80139)
Note: Some may find this performance *too energetic* (I believe this is the way Mozart would perform it). For something lighter and less energetic, try Sir Neville Marriner or Leonard Bernstein.

7. Serenade in B-flat "Gran Partita" K. 361
Sir Neville Marriner, conductor; Academy of St. Martin-in-the-Fields (Philips 4127262)

8. K. 216: Violin Concerto No. 3 in G major, and K. 219: Violin Concerto No. 5 in A major
Itzhak Perlman, violin; James Levine, conductor (Deutsche Grammophon 4100202)

9. String Quartets Nos. 14-23 K. 387, K. 421, K. 428, K. 458, K. 464, K. 465, K. 499, K. 575, K. 589, K. 590
   Alban Berg Quartet (TELDEC)

10. K. 492: *Le nozze di Figaro* (The Marriage of Figaro)
    Cast: Taddei, Schwarzkopf, Moffo, Cossotto; Conductor: Carlo Maria Giulini (EMI 5099973595922) Note: This is an early recording. James Levine's Metropolitan Opera modern recording with Kiri Te Kanawa is also excellent.

11. K. 527: *Don Giovanni*
    Cast: Wixell, Roni, Arroyo, Burrows, Te Kanawa; Conductor: Sir Colin Davis (Philips 4225412)

12. K. 620: *Die Zauberflöte* (The Magic Flute)
    Cast: Moll, Schreier, Adam Ude, Serra; Director: Sir Colin Davis (Philips 4225432)
    Note: Vol. 43 in Philips "The Complete Mozart Edition." Expensive new but very cheap used. Worth seeking out.

* * *

OPERA DVD RECORDINGS

If you are inclined to watch Mozart's seven major operas on DVD, here are my recommendations. Many of them have excerpts that can be previewed on YouTube.

First, if price is the primary concern, then you can't beat this three-opera package of inspired performances:

Le nozze di Figaro, Don Giovanni, and *Die Zauberflöte*
amazon.com/Mozart-Giovanni-Zauberflote-nozze-Figaro/dp/B00NCZ971S/

If you can buy them individually, here are my seven recommendations:

1. K. 366: *Idomeneo, re di Creta (Idomeneo, King of Create)*
   amazon.com/Mozart-Idomeneo-Remastered-Luciano-Pavarotti/dp/B000E5KOJI/

The Metropolitan Opera version with Pavarotti in the title role and James Levine conducting is very good, although many disagree that this is the best performance. Be sure to preview it on YouTube. The used price is a great deal.

2. K. 384: *Die Entführung aus dem Serail (The Abduction from the Harem)*
amazon.com/Mozart-Entfuhrung-Serail-Abduction-Seraglio/dp/B0009I8PHS/
This German-Language opera was filmed in Munich in 1980 with Karl Böhm conducting the Orchester Der Bayerischen Staatsoper.

3. K. 492: *Le nozze di Figaro (The Marriage of Figaro)*
amazon.com/Nozze-di-Figaro-Blu-ray/dp/B0013HA838/
A widely praised 2006 production with Antonio Pappano conducting the Orchestra of the Royal Opera House in London.

4. K. 527: *Don Giovanni*
amazon.com/Wolfgang-Amadeus-Mozart-Kringelborn-Metropolitan/dp/B003MSYXMS/
The Metropolitan Opera version designed by Franco Zeffirelli and conducted by James Levine, in October 2000, is expensive but well worth it.

5. K. 588: *Cosi Fan Tutte (Thus Do They All)*
amazon.com/Mozart-Cosi-Tutte-Miah-Persson/dp/B000NIWI9K/
The Glyndebourne Festival Opera in England is famous for their Mozart operas, and this one is no exception. Ivan Fischer conducts this great 2006 performance.

6. K. 620: *Die Zauberflöte* **(The Magic Flute):**
amazon.com/Mozart-Die-Zauberflöte-Magic-Flute/dp/B000050X31/
The Metropolitan Opera version designed by David Hockney and conducted by James Levine, in December 2000, is visually stunning and musically great.

7. K. 621: *La Clemenza di Tito (The Clemency of Titus)*
amazon.com/Mozart-Clemenza-Tito-Cambreling-
national/dp/B00X88FG50/
No great DVD recording of this overshadowed opera
currently exists, but Amazon Prime members can stream
the 2005 National Opera of Paris version for free.

* * *

EDUCATIONAL RECORDINGS

Bernstein, Leonard. (1973.) *The Unanswered Question: Six
Talks at Harvard by Leonard Bernstein.* Six DVDs. West Long
Branch, NJ: Kultur.

Bernstein's *tour de force* Norton Lectures at Harvard
University offer over 13 hours of viewing across six
lectures. He is a natural teacher who approaches music
in terms of rhetoric, linguistics, and poetry. It helps that
he conducts his own orchestra to illustrate his points.

These powerful, scholarly lectures can deepen your
understanding of music as a language. Best viewed in
small doses. The first two lectures use musical examples
from Mozart's Symphony No. 40 in G minor, K. 550.
Available on YouTube (see *Appendix: Online Music,
Films, Lectures*).

Courses by Robert Greenberg at **TheGreatCourses.com**

Robert Greenberg is also a great teacher, who has more
courses with The Teaching Company than any other
professor. He is witty and brilliant and can take you as
deep as you want to go into classical music.

Appendix

Mozart's Four-Star Compositions

from the *Pegasus Pocket Guide to Mozart:*

Symphonies

K. 504: *Symphony No. 38 in D* (Prague)

K. 543: *Symphony No. 39 in E-flat*

K. 550: *Symphony No. 40 in G minor*

K. 551: *Symphony No. 41 in C* (Jupiter)

Concertos

K. 459: *Piano Concerto No. 19 in F*

K. 466: *Piano Concerto No. 20 in D minor*

K. 467: *Piano Concerto No. 21 in C*

K. 491: *Piano Concerto No. 24 in C minor*

K. 503: *Piano Concerto No. 25 in C*

K. 595: *Piano Concerto No. 27 in B-flat*

K. 364: *Sinfonia Concertante in E-flat*

K. 622: *Clarinet Concerto in A*

Wind Ensemble Music

K. 361: *Serenade No. 10 in B-flat for Winds*

K. 388: *Serenade No. 12 in C minor for Winds*

Chamber Music

K. 465: *String Quartet No. 19 in C* (Dissonance)

K. 515: *String Quintet No. 2 in C*

K. 516: *String Quintet No. 3 in G minor*

K. 563: *Divertimento in E-flat for string trio*

Piano Ensemble Music

K. 452: *Piano and Wind Quintet in E-flat*

K. 478: *Piano Quartet in G minor*

Keyboard Music

K. 310: *Piano Sonata No. 8 in A minor*

K. 511: *Rondo in A minor*

K. 540: *Adagio in B minor*

K. 497: *Sonata in F* (Duet)

K. 608: *Fantasia in F minor for mechanical organ*

Church and Choral Music

K. 427: *Mass in C minor*

K. 626: *Requiem in D minor*

Operas

K. 366: *Idomeneo, re di Creta*

K. 492: *Le nozze di Figaro*

K. 527: *Don Giovanni*

K. 588: *Cosi fan tutte*

K. 620: *Die Zauberflöte*

Arias

K. 383: *"Nehmt meinen Dank"*

K. 418: *"Vorrei spiegarvi"*

About the Author

Mark Andre Alexander has a B.A. in English and an M.A. in Organization and Management Development. He works in Silicon Valley helping people take their next step. He has delivered training to engineering managers from around the world on High Performance Thinking.

He's a happy soul, a composer and musician, and likes to make people laugh.

Occasionally he publishes articles and books. He's married to a woman who improves him just by being present, and he believes everyone is on a journey to learn how to give and receive divine love.

Go to **MarkAndreAlexander.Com** to access a free 36-day course on *Creating Your Life.*

Subscribe to the "Creating Your Life" channel on YouTube.

THE SCHOOL OF
PYTHAGORAS™

Mozart's music is excellent because it still lives,
because he heard directly the sound current of God.
Harold Klemp

www.ingramcontent.com/pod-product-compliance
Lightning Source LLC
Chambersburg PA
CBHW071854020426
42331CB00010B/2519